Designing a Document Strategy

Designing a Document Strategy

Kevin Craine

MC² Books
Hurst, Texas

MC² Books is a member of the McGrew + McDaniel Group

Jacket Design by Tamara Grigsby

Illustrations by Talana Gamah

First Printing, September 2000

The author and publisher have made every effort to ensure the accuracy of the information and examples shown in this book. However, this book is sold without any warranty, expressed or implied. Neither the author nor the publisher will be liable for any damages caused or alleged to be caused by the inforamtion in this book. The opinions expressed in this book are those of the authors and not necessarily those of the publisher, booksellers or distributors.

MC² Books are available at special discounts for bulk purchases. Please contact McGrew + McDaniel Group, 860 W. Airport Freeway, Suite 709, Hurst, Texas 76054 or call +1 817 577 8984.

Find us on the web at http://www.mcgrewmcdaniel.com/

For McKenzie and Austin

Contents

Preface

We are in the age of a *document renaissance*. Never before in human history have we had so many ways to communicate. We've gone from cave drawings to fax machines, from parchment to PC's, from tribal legends to the global village of the World Wide Web. Never before have people reached so far or had such freedom to create, share and express information. Throughout this continuous change there has been one constant, and that's the Document. Whether constructed with hieroglyphs or hypertext, the Document has been a constant aide to human communication. It was there with the Unas at Giza. It was there with Moses at Mt. Sinai. It was there with Lincoln at Gettysburg.

Despite this lineage, the Document has been overshadowed in the recent computer technology explosion. Most of our attention has been on the sexier side of technology. But as technology guides us into an epoch where people demand access to information directly through computers, databases and the Internet, the complexion of the document has changed. Our traditional notions may no longer apply.

Technology, however, is not a cure-all. Old World communication artistry – how to assemble and present information for people – is still as valuable today as it was in the days of Homer. Indeed, the allure of technology has stranded us against the rocks more than once. Finding our way to improvements, efficiencies and savings in these waters will require that we navigate not only with the knowledge of how things work technically, but also with an understanding of the fundamental role documents play in communication between people. Those underlying facets can be translated into valuable improvements in the way we do business.

Most organizations do not consider themselves to be in the document business. Nevertheless, documents are a second venture for nearly all organizations. Without mounds of envelopes leaving mailrooms daily, most corporations would cease to exist. Without the unsung business forms of forgotten departmental functions, work processes would halt faster than a mouse-click. Without booklets, brochures, manuals, catalogs, checks, statements, invoices, ID cards, and the rest, businesses would simply see no business at all.

Documents are also the pavement of the information superhighway. Web pages, e-mail and electronic commerce all rely on documents as the medium that translates information into action. Whether printed on paper or displayed on a computer screen, documents prompt people to act and workers to work. Documents are a foundation of business revenue (and expense).

By leveraging information contained in documents, communicating effectively and reducing costs, firms that have a document-centric focus are more likely to have an advantage in the Information Age. To gain this advantage many organizations are attempting to design and implement a document strategy.

But developing a document strategy is not easy. The aspects to consider are wide-ranging, complicated and elusive. I have observed many individuals who are both inspired *and* frustrated by discussions concerning a document strategy. Their inspiration tends to fade, however, while their frustration remains. The decision to develop a document strategy can be a paralyzing one and often the quandary becomes, "I know a document strategy is important, but how do I *develop* one?"

Existing answers to this question are either purely technical or primarily conceptual in nature. While jargon and theory can bring to light aspects that one must understand or consider when designing a document strategy, they do not bring the would-be implementer any closer to actually *doing* anything to put the theory into practice. What is missing is a process to follow that will guide decisions and actions that result in an effective strategy.

This book provides a formula to aid in the translation of concepts and technology into bottom-line improvements. My hope is to fill the gap between theory and practice, inspire the reader in the most important areas to consider, and provide a process that will frame a meaningful strategy.

This book is written for managers, technicians and consultants who want to develop a document strategy but aren't sure how to go about it. Assuming the reader has experience in the field of information technology, a certain amount of jargon specific to the document industry is used. But one need not possess a degree in computer science or years of experience in dreary data centers or dusty print shops to find this book a useful tool in the development of an effective document strategy.

The techniques presented are tailored specifically for those in the document business yearning for a process to follow. My intent, however, is not to provide all the answers in a cookie-cutter strategy, but rather to prompt informed decisions and thoughtful actions toward specific improvement goals. I do not suggest that this is the best or only way to craft a document strategy, but the principles have proven effective in several disciplines including Total Quality Management, Organizational Development, Data Processing and Communications.

A document strategy will vary for each organization. Some customizing of this work is a must, and I encourage readers to transform the approach into actions that are appropriate for his or her particular situation.

Kevin Craine

kevin@document-strategy.com

Acknowledgements

The creation of this book would not have been possible without the assistance of several people whose encouragement and suggestions made this a far better book than it might otherwise have been. First and foremost, I am indebted to Paul Telles, a knowledgeable and consistent editor, who was vital in the creation of this work. My thanks also to Pat McGrew and Bill McDaniel for their unwavering motivation and support. Leslie Smid provided valuable information, inspiration and encouragement. Dr. Bonita Kolb of Marylhurst University provided important guidance during the birth of this project. Dr. Michael Turton was also helpful in the initial stages of development. Richard Burket, David Carlson, Lisa Magnuson, Tammy Rivas and Sandra Strait provided constructive feedback at crucial points during the writing process. Thanks also to Brittney and Dave Asher, as well as the staff at the Shoen library on the Marylhurst campus who silently ignored my lurking in their quiet, book-filled sanctuary.

Several industry colleagues agreed to be interviewed during my initial research: Debbie Cannon, Toby Cobrin, Dr. Keith Davidson, Tom Martino, Keith Nickoloff and Mark Wahl. I must also acknowledge my colleagues at Regence BlueCross BlueShield of Oregon and *Document Processing Technology* magazine. The descriptions and convictions expressed herein represent my own opinion, however, and do not necessarily represent the views of my employers.

These acknowledgments would not be complete without expressing my gratitude and love to all my family – in particular my father Martin who was my personal editor from start to finish. Above all, I thank my wife Allyson who challenged me "be brilliant" on countless occasions. Finally, I am grateful for my children, McKenzie and Austin, for their innocent understanding while Dad closeted himself away from their world to work on the book.

1

Introduction

In early human history, primitive tribes documented the movement of bison on cavern walls and outcroppings of rock. The tribesmen painstakingly scribed pictograms in the sediment with stones and bones. The location and timing of the herd's arrival was vital information that could mean the difference between a successful hunt and hungry days of wandering through the wilderness. Information alone, however, did not feed the clan. It was only after the hunters took the information from the cave walls and converted it into action – by finding and killing their prey – that their families were fed.

Fast-forward 40 thousand years to an age where information is shared instantaneously and effortlessly around the globe. Digital information drives the machinery of modern society: currency and stock exchange; health care administration and medical treatment; government, military and civilian operations. Information alone, however, will not nourish a nation. It is only after information is productively used – by prompting meaningful actions – that society is served.

Whether in the Stone Age or the Information Age, information is of little value if it is not converted into the right kinds of action.

Documents Convert Information into Action

Human communication has been the catalyst for the Information Age. Computers, databases, networks and printers – the aggregation of information technology in modern organizations – are put into place to gather, distill and present information for people. People take this information and act in some way. It is the gap between information and action that is key. All of the gadgets, widgets and wires in the world are for naught if this gap is not effectively crossed. Consider the word *communication*. It is based on the Latin *commun*, or common, and the suffix "ie" which means "to make or do." So one meaning of communication is to make information common between people who then make or do something. Documents do this.

Communication is a human penchant that defined Homo sapiens as people. We are now more likely to communicate using hypertext than hieroglyphs, but the basic function remains the same: to make information common between people, who then act in some way. How can our documents take the information we have gathered and communicate it in a way that elicits the desired response from our readers? These "desired reactions" are at the very heart of how documents are strategic.

Documents are Strategic

Designing a document strategy starts with the notion that documents convert information into action. Are readers inspired to buy our products or engage our services? Are people prompted to act efficiently and correctly within the inner workings of our business processes? Have people understood our message and adopted our point of view?

Documents have great scope and importance because they provoke a variety of actions critical to an organization's business processes. Companies communicate with customers through documents. Documents drive revenue by prompting customers to buy, borrow and pay. Customer satisfaction, brand recognition and perceived quality are fostered by documents that communicate clearly, provide accurate and timely information, and serve the needs of readers.

Documents are also the beginning and end of internal business processes. They are the tools that help run a business every day. Documents connect work groups and link key business processes to the people who perform and manage those processes. The efficiency of day-to-day workflow hinges on action provoked by documents. Do workers get the right information when they need it and then act accordingly? Are they wasting time searching for information and correcting errors? Are they besieged with useless information and weighted down by unending paperwork?

Documents can influence the way people think and feel. Corporate documents inspire a feeling about the company that issues them and influence what customers think about the quality – good or bad – of products and services. Political candidates, social activists and religious groups use documents to sway opinion and persuade people to adopt a certain point of view or behavior. Law enforcement and governmental agencies use documents to record public opinion, establish societal norms and influence the conduct of citizens. For students and scholars, documents help to convert information into understanding and learning.

Documents are Tactical

If a document strategy starts with the notion that documents convert information into action, then it ends with the recognition that documents are a tactical liability if they are not effective. Whether digital or paper, documents cost money to produce and require labor to process.

Consider the following statistics:

- Thirty billion original documents are used each year in the United States.[1]

- The cost of documents to corporate America is estimated to reach as much as 15 percent of annual corporate revenue.[2]

- Documents claim up to 60 percent of office worker's time and account for up to 45 percent of labor costs.[3]

- 85 percent of documents are never retrieved, 50 percent are duplicates, and 60 percent are obsolete. [4]

- For every dollar that a company spends for a final document, ten dollars are spent to manage the process.[5]

Given these figures, it's no surprise that the lion's share of work concerning documents is focused on producing pages faster and cheaper – or not at all. A quintessential charter of any document strategy must be to cut operating cost, reduce labor and eliminate waste. The success of a document strategy will certainly be measured using these factors as a yardstick.

It is natural, then, that there is no shortage of technology available to address the market posed by the tactical aspects of document processing. Indeed, entire industry segments have been spawned as a result. Without a strategic viewpoint, however, it is easy to mistake the latest technological advancement for a meaningful strategy. The danger is to allow planning to be clouded by the technical miasma of gadgetry and marketing hype.

Another constraint that must be overcome by those designing a document strategy is that the traditional view of documents is tactical rather than strategic. Documents are generally seen as a problem or a liability, not an opportunity or an asset. But simply viewing documents tactically – a cost to be contained or a function to out-source – limits opportunity to incremental improvements whenever they happen to present themselves and excludes a large part of the equation.

For this reason, it is imperative to design your document strategy with a balanced perspective: documents are both a strategic asset and a tactical liability.

A Document Strategy Requires Balance

For a bird to fly it must have two wings. A document strategy also requires two wings: one strategic and one tactical. How documents inspire people to act, what those actions are and how those actions serve business objectives are aspects of the strategic wing of an effective plan. Concerns on the tactical side include cost reduction, efficient use of labor and return on investments in technology and facilities.

Wings enable flight, but it takes balance to soar. A document strategy must balance the strategic aspects of documents with the tactical realities that are inescapable in today's business environment. A document strategy architect must design a plan with the notion that documents convert information into action, along with the understanding that documents are a liability if they fail in this premise. An over-emphasis on either "wing" will limit opportunity. You may need to fly a little to the left, or a little to the right, depending on which way the wind blows or where the opportunities are found. The ultimate success of your document strategy depends on the balance used in your approach.

Using Documents Strategically means

Using Information Strategically

Organizations must adopt a document strategy if for no other reason than the current exponential growth of information. More information has been produced in the last thirty years than in the previous five thousand – the entire history of civilization.[6] What's more, that body of information is expected to double in less than five years.[7] With over 90 percent of information contained in documents,[8] it is clear that whatever the medium – pixels or paper, bytes or birch bark – documents are the currency of human communication. Information: You've got to be able to find it, you've got to be able to use it, and you've got to be able to keep it. Documents allow us to do all these things.

Growth of Information

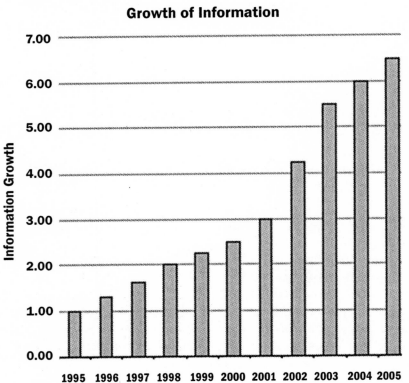

For most organizations, documents compose much, if not all, of the product they sell or the service they provide. A health insurance company, for example, does not provide diagnosis or treatment, only information about what doctor is available, what coverage is provided and what claims have been paid. For companies such as this, documents *are* the product – the only tangible evidence of the service provided.

If firms are not competitive in using the information they have within their enterprise, they will be less able to face the competitive pressures of changing markets, shrinking margins and increasing competition. Companies must have *information agility* in order to effectively react to dynamic changes in their marketplace. Traditionally, change in the marketplace was somewhat predictable; business increased or decreased in a reasonably linear pattern and competitors entered or exited the market in a relatively logical and predictable fashion. Today, however, the economic, technological and societal factors that influence change are moving simultaneously and unpredictably. A document strategy ensures that an organization can find, use and keep information with agility and effectiveness.

Information is now the most valuable component of the entire economic chain, according to Peter Drucker, the prominent management consultant. Organizations that are able to harness the power of information and manage, share and use information effectively are well positioned to create value for everyone involved, says Drucker.[9]

But the cost of harnessing that value is high. Investment in information technology now accounts for over one-half of the United States' gross investment in equipment.[10] It has been estimated that U.S. businesses spend more than $100 billion on hardware alone.[11] Documents are a vehicle that can turn the expense of gathering information into an asset. They are one aspect of information processing that can be quantifiably measured and improved. A document strategy is vital because it monitors, directs and improves the way information is used in a very tangible way. Improvements made in document systems can ultimately determine the real value of the information you have gathered and the technology used to collect it.

A Document is a Document

One stumbling block for document strategists is the very definition of a document. The accepted definition is constantly evolving, and our traditional view of documents as strictly paper no longer applies in today's wired world. The modern view of the Document is expanding to include an ever-widening scope. This can be troublesome when defining the reach of your document strategy. Is a document defined in terms of the media that carries the information – paper vs. digital? Or are documents defined by the role they play – bills, brochures, books, etc? Should voice mails, e-mails, Web pages and video clips be considered documents? What separates a document from the multitude of information carrying files in an organization?

Whatever your definition, it is important to remember that the defining characteristics of a document have not changed over time and are not dependent upon the medium, content or method of delivery. Just as a rose by any other name would smell as sweet, a document by any other medium would be as winsome.

Are Documents Paper or Digital?

Despite the popular notion of the "paperless office," the Information Age is actually powering a boom in paper. Since 1984 – the dawn of the personal computer – the number of pages printed by American companies has grown by 500 percent to over 1.5 trillion pages per year. This equates to a mountain of paper 6,500 times taller than Mount Everest.[12]

In 1995, only about 10 percent of documents were presented in digital form. Predictions point to an eventual decline in paper documents, however, to about 30 percent of total by 2005. It is important to note that the predicted growth of information rises considerably over the same time period. As a result, the number of printed pages will actually double by 2005.[13]

Paper has staying power because people find it reassuring. Paper is tangible; something you can put your hands on as opposed to a virtual document somewhere. It is really a matter of comfort and confidence. Other than devoted technophiles, most people are less likely to soak in the bathtub with a PC than they are with a magazine or newspaper. And people often lack the confidence in technology to access documents when they need them. If it is something important, chances are you are going to print it. There are few Ph.D. candidates, for instance, that don't have several copies of their dissertation printed on paper and safely tucked away.

In the corporate world, many people still need to work with physical rather than virtual documents. One reason for this is that more than 60 percent of organizations still process, store and retrieve documents manually.[14] While many organizations will eventually adopt digital documents, many have elected to

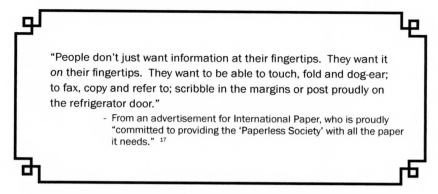

"People don't just want information at their fingertips. They want it *on* their fingertips. They want to be able to touch, fold and dog-ear; to fax, copy and refer to; scribble in the margins or post proudly on the refrigerator door."

- From an advertisement for International Paper, who is proudly "committed to providing the 'Paperless Society' with all the paper it needs." [17]

hold back in order to learn from the efforts of early pioneers and wait until the risks of conversion are negligible.

Nevertheless, the tenacity of paper does not displace the evidence that digital documents are an important tool for doing business. The Internet, for instance, provides nearly boundless access to customers, and companies are jumping on the e-commerce bandwagon. A recent poll of 371 chief financial officers conducted by Duke University reports that 56 percent of the executives surveyed plan to sell their products over the Internet. This sentiment is growing, up from 24 percent in 1998.[15]

Those designing a document strategy must confront the coexistence of paper and digital documents for the foreseeable future. One indicator is the surprisingly slow adoption rate of Internet billing by customers. According to Robert Kunio, vice president of Global Technology Development for Moore Corporation, less than one percent of the customers of those corporations that have embraced Internet billing have asked to stop receiving their paper bills. "The sponsors of these business plans are, at the very least, embarrassed," says Kunio. "Based on this slow migration rate, paper and e-bills will most likely coexist for years to come."[16] It will take more time for customers to develop comfort and confidence using digital documents. Regardless of the timing, the transition into the digital world of documents will not be made without building upon the legacy of paper documents. A savvy document strategist must look for ways to re-purpose paper documents to populate new digital systems and continue to seek improvements in the handling of documents using P.O.P. – plain old paper.

Where Does a Document Strategy Fit in the Corporate Picture?

Corporate

IT

Document

Documents play a significant role in nearly every business strategy or initiative. Therefore, documents should be given the same attention in strategic planning as other important aspects of business such as marketing, finance, human resources and information technology. A document-centric focus that is sensibly linked to organizational objectives can mean the difference between the success and failure of other important business plans. It is no longer enough for organizations to plan and implement strategies in isolation from the Document. The challenge, as Peter Senge puts it, is to "think systemically and act holistically,"[18] and organizations must adopt a more inclusive view of documents by recognizing them as a vehicle to bring alignment and success to their entire agenda of business strategies and objectives. Otherwise, the lack of this type of strategic alignment will give rise to problems that will affect the overall profitability of the firm.

Consider these three major strategies within an organization:

- Corporate strategy
- Information Technology (IT) strategy
- Document strategy

These strategies are highly interdependent and important in the overall success of any enterprise. Their misalignment can result in increased costs, decreased profits and unsatisfied customers.[19]

Corporate Strategy

Since before the Industrial Age, the bottom-line corporate objective has been to make a profit. But making a profit is no longer the only aspect of doing business that is important. Today, organizations must also take into account additional factors of how they do business. As a result of the Total Quality Management movement, many organizations now regard the satisfaction of their customers as the measure of success that will ultimately determine their profitability. Others have learned the importance of efficient and effective workflow, and that efficiency is not always guaranteed by the purchase of the latest technology. Forward-looking firms also recognize that information is a vital asset and key to finding real return from investments in technology, facilities and people.

While profit will remain paramount, these additional aspects of corporate strategy play a crucial role in determining the proper alignment between information technology and document strategies.

IT Strategy

In the 1970s and 1980s, information technology (IT) strategies were single-minded. They focused on simply gathering, processing and outputting data. With the advent of high-speed laser printers, however, *data* processing professionals unwittingly entered the world of *document* processing – a world hitherto inhabited only by typesetters, graphic artists and pressmen. A gap developed between the advancement of

City Utilities
123 City Street
City, State 12345-1234

```
Billing Date:  4/5/01
Last month electrical usage/KW:  420
Last month bill:  $78.21
Last payment received:  $29.87
Current month electrical usage/KW:310
Current month bill:  $61.22

Please pay current and outstanding
amounts by the 15th of the month.
To make a donation to City Parks
Fund add 50 cents.
```

information technology and the cosmetic appearance of corporate documents. Even today, countless documents continue to be issued that look scarcely different than if they had been typed on a typewriter.

How could this happen in light of the tremendous advancements in printer technology? The answer lies in the misalignment between corporate, IT, and document strategies. Until only recently, IT objectives could be summed simply: produce the right data at the right time. The effectiveness of the documents produced was not a concern. Does this mean that data processing professionals were insensitive to the needs of the organization? No. Effective documents simply were not part of the paradigm of the computer department.

Document Strategy

What single aspect of business is critical to profitability yet "owned" by no one? The answer is: the Document. After all, most organizations have an IT director, but how many have a "document director?" The result is a proliferation of documents that do not effectively serve corporate objectives. How often do you receive a statement that doesn't make sense, a bill that is inaccurate or misleading, or a letter that is confusing? How often do you find yourself searching for information in multiple places, using duplicate forms or sifting through obsolete files? When you open your mail, are you made to feel that your patronage is important or the products that you buy are of good quality? The trouble is that no one has responsibility for what these documents look like or how effectively they communicate.

To see the consequences of this situation, imagine an overall corporate strategy that includes these three basic elements:

- Increase Revenue
- Decrease Costs
- Increase Customer Satisfaction

If documents going to external customers are daunting or confusing, and communication is unclear, what will be the effect on these basic corporate objectives? One consequence is that customers may either be late with their payments

or not pay at all. The result: *revenue will decrease*. Instead
of paying, customers may call the company for clarification.
The result: *costs will increase*. Eventually, customers may
become frustrated and angry about the way the company does
business. The result: *satisfaction will decrease*. What will be
seen in the end is a total reversal of the fundamental corporate
objectives.

Consider the consequences when looking at internal processes.
In this case, corporate strategy may be:

- Decrease Effort
- Increase Productivity
- Reduce Labor (headcount)

If internal documents are misleading, hard to find, outdated or
inaccurate, what will be the effect on work processes? Workers
will make mistakes, waste time looking for needed information
and require additional supervision. The result: *more effort will
be required*. Instead of being more productive, employees will
be continually re-working their tasks. The result: *productivity
will decrease*. Eventually, additional staff will be needed to
maintain the business. The result: *headcount will increase*. This
is, again, a total reversal of corporate objectives.

In most organizations today the IT department continues to
focus solely on processing data and delivering *output*. Even
trendy business-to-business and Web-based initiatives tend to
focus more on technology than on communication. When
viewed from a *document* perspective, however, the negative
consequences to a corporation can be clearly seen. Most
corporate strategies, however, have traditionally overlooked
documents as a factor that drives daily business. As a result,
vital documents may perform exactly opposite from their
intended purpose. What is needed is a document strategy
to properly align corporate and IT strategies around the key
objectives of the firm.

Alignment of Strategies

The essential questions are: What is your corporate strategy
and how can your document strategy support it? What are the
IT strategies needed to enable both?

Like any fundamental business strategy, a document strategy must be addressed at several levels. As far as customers are concerned, the factors that determine satisfaction and perceived quality are most apparent through external documents. As far as workers are concerned, routine interdepartmental documents enable efficient workflow and provide "corporate knowledge." Both of these aspects are of fundamental importance to corporate profitability.

How we manage documents has a great deal to do with how we manage business. A document strategy can help make documents part of the success of a business rather than one of the problems. Yet, only 25 percent of companies have a document strategy.[20] This book describes a much-needed method for putting one into place.

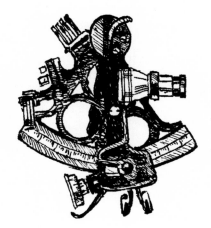

2

Applying the Document Strategy Model

Once you decide to implement a document strategy, it is easy to become paralyzed by the complexity of the decision. The evolving role of documents, the complications of technology, and the politics of corporate culture and change all conspire to make your task seem overwhelming. The vista of your document strategy can seem boundless. Navigating with a balance of strategic vision and tactical common sense is not easy without a clear map to provide direction. This can result in *Blank Page Syndrome* – a crippling affliction for a document strategist – where the blank page looms gravely, ideas retreat to the farthest corner of inspiration and the expectations of management become seemingly unobtainable.

Faced with the enormity of designing a document strategy, it is tempting to look to hardware, software or the Internet for a shrink-wrapped solution. This approach is bound to fall short, however. Technology is only part of the equation and its purchase and deployment must be guided with an understanding of the role documents play in your organization and the needs of the people who use them.

Even if you recognize the importance of a document strategy, the question remains: *How do I go about developing one?* The answer to this question is not universal because different organizations will require different document strategies. What is needed most is a *process* to guide the development of your strategy so that it is meaningful, practical and ensures worthwhile and lasting results.

Characteristics of the Process

Comprehensive, yet manageable. The process of designing a document strategy must be comprehensive enough to ensure that something important is not overlooked. It must also be manageable enough to avoid the risk of a project so large and slow that nothing ever gets done. At one end of the spectrum, a "just do it" approach runs the risk that inadequate planning will lead to wasted effort. At the other end of the range, an overly broad approach can invite "scope creep" and result in a project where objectives become moving targets and decisions come slowly (if at all). Strike a balance between the two by focusing your efforts on those areas that are the most important and the most likely to bring about worthwhile improvement. Consider the "80/20" rule: it is likely that 80 percent of improvements can be found by concentrating on 20 percent of the overall scope.

Linked to company goals. Ultimately, the real test of your document strategy will be its effect on the performance of your company. Does your strategy decrease operating costs and increase opportunities for revenue? Does it increase customer satisfaction? Does it serve executive vision? For your document strategy to appear on the corporate "radar screen" and gain support it must bring about benefit and improvement in those areas that are of fundamental importance to your firm.

Clearly demonstrated measurements. Measuring and demonstrating improvement is critical for the ongoing success of your document strategy. The adage *you can improve only that* *which you can measure* holds true. Measurements help answer three essential questions: Where are you now? Where do you want to go? How will you know you have arrived? Once your plan has been put into place, measurements help demonstrate, in a quantifiable way, the results of your improvement efforts.

Addresses corporate culture. One very influential factor that is often avoided or overlooked is the influence of corporate culture on the design and outcome of a document strategy. Internal politics, lack of support and resistance to change are all difficult and elusive factors that can quickly kill your document strategy. The questions are: How do you *sell* your document strategy? How will people react to the changes you propose? Will the culture of your organization help your efforts or hinder your progress? The design of your strategy must account for the cultural tides of your organization and look for ways to swim with the current rather than against the flow.

Facilitates implementation and evaluates results. The most well-conceived strategies are of little value if they are not executed effectively. To develop a vision is not enough. For your document strategy to be of practical value it must facilitate specific actions to achieve specific goals. Once those actions are put into place, evaluation and re-measurement are vital because the success of your strategy is known only if it can be demonstrated.

The Document Strategy Model

With these basic characteristics in mind, consider the Document Strategy Model as one approach to the design of a document strategy. This model is a useful guide and has five elements as a framework.

The Document Strategy Model is *not* intended to be linear. The overlapping circles of the model demonstrate that the steps will often overlap. You might find that you don't need to follow every step in detail or there are times when you must retrace your steps back to square one. The framework can and should be adapted to suit your particular situation, organization or requirement. The Document Strategy Model helps to provide focus, avoid pitfalls and save valuable time and energy.

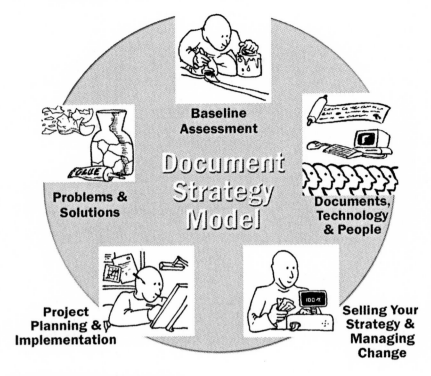

Document Strategy Model

- Baseline Assessment
- Documents, Technology & People
- Selling Your Strategy & Managing Change
- Project Planning & Implementation
- Problems & Solutions

Baseline Assessment

The process starts with a Baseline Assessment that asks: Where are you, and where do you need to go? The assessment helps you "get located" by establishing a baseline about the purpose and direction of your organization, the needs, pressures and constraints it must satisfy and manage, and the hard numbers that measure its success. You will ask questions like:

- What needs must be satisfied? What pressures and constraints must be managed?

- What are the most important measures of your performance?

- What are your most important objectives?

- What are the initiatives underway to achieve those goals?

- What is your core business – your reason for being?

- How does your organization envision success?

Although these questions may seem simple, the answers are not always obvious. If you have any doubt, try the following experiment with the next five co-workers you meet. Ask each person to give a one-sentence answer to each of the questions above. Once you have gathered all their answers you will likely find significant disagreement in the responses.

A Baseline Assessment also explores the most pressing problems that challenge your company and the most advantageous opportunities for improvement.

Documents, Technology and People

One way to keep your document strategy manageable is to view it through three basic frames of reference: documents, technology and people. At the most fundamental level, this is what a document strategy is all about. Documents are the subject of your strategy, technology is how you produce them, and people are why they exist.

- Which documents are most vital to the success of your organization?

- What technology is used to create them?

- Who are the people who use and care about these documents?

You will chart a meaningful course for your strategy by compiling a list of target documents, assessing how those documents are produced, and understanding the needs of the people who use and care about them.

Problems and Solutions

In order to be successful, your document strategy must provide solutions to the problems in your current processes. It is impossible to determine appropriate solutions until you understand and define the problems that exist. You will do this by comparing how things are with the way they should be. You will examine how your current processes perform and determine whether or not they perform in ways that meet the needs of your organization. Once you have defined the problems that exist and determined their root cause(s), you will identify and select the best solutions to solve those problems and improve your processes.

- How does your document process *really* perform?

- How *should* the process perform in order to meet your needs and requirements?

- What problems prevent your document process from performing adequately, and why do they exist?

- How will you solve the problems you discover and make improvements to your process?

- What is the best solution among the many that may be available?

Selling your Strategy and Managing Change

Next, the Document Strategy Model explores the critical need to sell your strategy and manage change. Your efforts are not likely to be successful if you do not enlist the support of decision-makers and co-workers. Selling your strategy requires a solid business case as well as the ability to "speak the language" of the people you aim to convince. You will do this by constructing a financial analysis and a formal proposal for your ideas and solutions. You will also examine ways to enlist the support of co-workers and decision-makers.

Change and corporate culture significantly influence your document strategy. To better manage change you will explore the roles people play in a successful change initiative. You will also consider the natural and emotional reactions that people have during times of change. In addition, you will examine the cultural characteristics of your organization and how they will influence your efforts.

- How can you "sell" your document strategy to those who must approve and sponsor it?

- How will you get the support of your co-workers?

- How will people react to change?

- What is the prevailing culture of your organization?

- How will certain cultural characteristics influence the success of your strategy?

Project Planning and Implementation

 Project planning and implementation is where all of your assessment, analysis and planning must come together. You must develop a project plan that will be clearly understood by everyone involved and guide your efforts to a successful implementation. You must challenge your assumptions, test your solutions and demonstrate your success. Some of the questions you will answer are:

- How will you implement your strategy? Who must do what...how...and when?

- What are the objectives you seek? What must you "deliver" in order to be successful?

- What are the risks associated with your plans, and how will you mitigate those risks?

- How will you assess and demonstrate your success?

3

Baseline Assessment

A sailor must know two things before he can chart a course: his current location and the location of where he wants to go. Picking a destination may be easy – the Bahamas perhaps – but determining the precise distance and direction the ship must travel to get to the tropical paradise requires a skipper know his exact location at the time of his departure. During his journey, a navigator also must constantly measure his progress. Unexpected weather conditions, changes in ocean currents and breakdowns in equipment all conspire to throw him off course. To reach his destination safely and successfully requires an accurate assessment of the ship's progress compared to where it started from and where it needs to go.

When mapping a document strategy, you must also understand two things in order to make the right directional decisions: *Where are you now? Where do you want to go?* Ports of call may be easy to settle on – increase revenue, cut costs, satisfy customers – but to reach those destinations will require a reliable starting point from which to calculate the course of your plans. A document strategy also calls for consistent measurement of progress. Unexpected difficulties, changes in business climate and breakdowns in technology can work against even the most well- conceived plans. Reaching a meaningful destination requires that the progress of your document strategy be continuously evaluated – comparing where you are, with where you started and where you need to go.

Elements of a Baseline Assessment

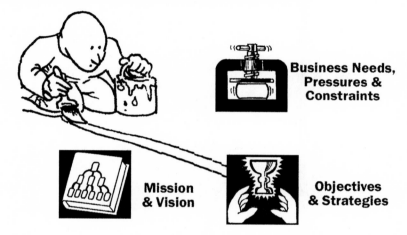

Business Needs, Pressures & Constraints

Mission & Vision

Objectives & Strategies

The first element of the Document Strategy Model is a Baseline Assessment. This assessment provides a starting point. It provides a sense of direction and helps to make the process of designing a document strategy more manageable and measurable. Most importantly, a Baseline Assessment makes certain that your plans are closely linked to the fundamental needs and objectives of your particular organization. The more closely your strategy is tied to these basics, the more likely it will be given sponsorship, support and funding, and the more likely your efforts will result in meaningful improvement.

Perform a Baseline Assessment in three steps:

Step 1. Understand the key *business needs, pressures and constraints* that your organization must satisfy and manage.

- What are the hard numbers that measure company performance?

- What are the business pressures that your company must manage?

- What are the constraints, requirements and expectations that your organization must live with each day?

Step 2. Examine the specific *objectives and strategies* that are defined in your company business plan.

- What are your long-term objectives and overall strategy?

- What are your organization's short-term objectives and operational strategies?

- What are the specific ways your company tracks the achievement of these objectives?

Step 3. Understand the *mission and vision* of your organization.

- What are the reasons your company exists?
- How does your company envision success?
- What are the specific initiatives underway to achieve your company's mission and vision?

By following these steps you will perform a comprehensive yet manageable assessment of your organization. With this balance, you will be in a better position to determine two essential pieces of information you need to chart your course: where you are, and where you need to go.

"Everybody starts from a baseline, and the baseline is today," says Toby Cobrin, technology advisor for Xplor International. "You have to understand today in order to shape tomorrow. Understand your business objectives first, and then search for the right technologies to meet those goals. A document strategy should take it's direction from the direction of the business." [1]

Having a meaningful direction is important because if you select the wrong processes to improve or the wrong the documents to reengineer, your efforts may be wasted. The process you choose to improve must be one that is critical to the successful achievement of your organization's goals. By doing an assessment you will be less likely to waste time and money on plans that do not contribute to the fundamental needs of your organization.

Imagine a chain of retail stores that, over several months, installs a sophisticated electronic forms system in each of its store locations. The aim is to change the way salespeople handle transactions and thereby increase customer satisfaction. At great expense and effort, each store is eventually brought online. The system works flawlessly. Each feature performs as promised. Success is declared. The trouble is that existing store customers have, for the most part, been happy with their in-store experience. They are already pleased with the service they receive. As a result, the "improvement" actually does nothing to help the company. The effort, time and money would have been better spent elsewhere. Indeed, the vision of store executives is more concerned with courting new customers over the Internet than with in-store sales. In this case, a Baseline Assessment would have set the pilots of this strategy in the correct direction. They would have understood "where they were" with respect to customer satisfaction and "where they needed to go" with respect to corporate vision.

> The notion of a baseline can be thought of in engineering terms. Surveyors begin from a base-line – a known and charted location – when making precise measurements and exact calculations. Engineers must know their exact starting point in order to determine the direction and distance of other target locations.

A Baseline Assessment guarantees that, by design, your document strategy will be closely linked to the fundamental needs and goals of your organization. Tom Martino, senior director of communications services for Warner-Lambert, stresses the value of viewing your strategy from a broad, organizational angle. "There is usually a better way of managing your documents than you currently have, especially if you look at it from a global perspective. We work early on to avoid overlooking something, then ask ourselves: Can we do anything?" [2]

This perspective is important because the people responsible for documents are, for the most part, isolated from policy-makers. Senior executives, strategic planners and corporate officers tend to run in different circles than data center directors, print shop managers and systems programmers. To gain a worthwhile perspective, you will need to do more than simply read the company mission statement or annual report. It will require a certain amount of investigation, questioning and research. Spend time to actively seek an understanding of the driving factors of your business.

Developing a document strategy can be overwhelming. One key to success is to find ways to make the process manageable. Your assessment will help you focus your strategy on those areas that are most important to your organization. As a result, you will make better decisions and more meaningful recommendations. You will be less likely to succumb to scope creep or overlook important opportunities. You will not be led off course by issues or conditions that have lesser bearing on your overall direction.

A Baseline Assessment is important, if for no other reason, because it is the first step in selling your strategy. The more effectively your strategy serves the real needs and goals of your organization, the more likely your plan will be given the resources, support and understanding it will need to be successful. Dr. Keith Davidson, president of Xplor International, puts it this way: "Without a good assessment you probably won't sell the idea of a document strategy. Groundwork is very influential. I've seen cases when lousy plans were given support simply because the analysis was so accurate and complete. Management said: 'This must be a good strategy.' Whether or not your solutions will be fruitful may not be as important initially as you shop for support. If your assessment is sound, executive management will be more likely to buy your plan." [3]

Analysis Paralysis

It seems cliché, but time is one commodity that no one seems to have enough of. And the thought of spending hour after hour in a conference room laboring over a drawn out assessment is enough to drive busy managers and overworked technicians down the street to the nearest Starbucks. Truth be told, most might enjoy the opportunity to more fully examine a difficult situation before launching into solutions, but the unfortunate question remains: Who has the time?

"I'm not a big believer in lengthy analysis," says P.C. McGrew, consultant and author of *Online Text Management*. "While it is important to look at each enterprise individually, and perhaps look at divisions and departments individually, I have found that a protracted assessment tends to do nothing more than delay things." [4]

Assessments have a garnered a bad reputation because they often fall victim to *analysis paralysis* – the disabling tendency to get distracted by detail. Analysis paralysis can spread quickly when technology is involved. Jargon and detail often unwittingly combine to bog down the assessment process and delay productive action. Assessments also become mired when they involve a number of different functions within an organization, and decisions require input from several different departments. "Decision by committee" can be as frustrating as it is fruitful. One tip to avoiding analysis paralysis is to accept, from the beginning, that there may be details that will need further consideration at a later time. Place these hanging issues aside for another day and don't let ancillary detail and technical minutia sidetrack your assessment. "Let the details fall into place later," says Leslie Smid, adjunct professor at the Oregon Graduate Institute of Science and Technology. "For now, get a good sense of things, but don't take forever." [5]

For most of us, the temptation to jump ahead to solutions is hard to resist – especially when the problem is clear and workable answers are available. Certainly, overblown assessments can waste time and sidetrack progress, but the "just do it" approach, while sometimes appropriate, can also result in "just do it again." Spending the time for a Baseline Assessment is perhaps your most profound investment of effort. Without a Baseline Assessment you will likely end up needing to back track later and do additional work – either to find justification for your idea, or to re-work solutions that missed the mark.

Step One: Business needs and pressures

 If you do nothing else with respect to conducting a Baseline Assessment, understand the business *needs, pressures and constraints* of your organization. Do this by performing a survey of these areas of concern that are common to most organizations.[6]

Hard Numbers. What are the hard and fast numbers that your organization uses to measure its performance? This may include numbers set forth in operating budgets, expected growth targets, anticipated rates of return, desired customer retention, containment of administrative costs, and so on. Other numbers to investigate are those that are reported to senior management and divisional vice presidents. Look at the figures found in quarterly financial reports and performance projections. Seek out statistics that measure corporate performance.

Competitive Pressures. What are the most important competitive pressures your company must manage? Start by understanding marketplace competitors and how they challenge the success of your company. How does your company aim to alleviate this competition? What are the plans to gain an advantage? What are current efforts with things like product development, advertising or market research? Look at resources like your annual report, corporate planning guides and product development announcements. Meeting agendas and budget guidelines can give you a valuable perspective. Ask managers, executives and project planners to explain their view of the business horizon. Look for connections between your firm's hard numbers and its competitive pressures. What areas measure up as strengths? What are weaknesses? How do these pressures influence the course of your strategy?

Competition is most often thought of as an external pressure, but internal competition should also be considered in your assessment. Internal competition is an important dynamic for any organization, but it is especially important during corporate restructuring, mergers and acquisitions. Examine the internal climate of your company. Will internal competition help or hinder your efforts? How are resources and funding allocated? What competitive constraints exist with respect to equipment, staffing and compensation?

Operational Pressures. The litmus test for most organizations is how well they face the pressures of conducting business every day. These challenges may include labor and workforce issues, difficulties with logistics and locations, poor product quality, material shortages or manufacturing snafus. One way to uncover specific operational pressures is to compare the hard numbers of a given department against the overall competitive pressures of your organization. What surfaces when you compare the two? What specific constraints exist? What operational pressures must be managed and/or mitigated?

Constraints, Requirements and Expectations. In addition to the needs and pressures of doing business, most firms must deal with constraints in the form of requirements and expectations. These constraints are, if not mandatory, important aspects of doing business that should not be overlooked. Government and regulatory agencies have very specific requirements (both international and domestic) that must be met. Commitments outlined in contracts, settlements and agreements are another set of requirements that mandate certain performance. Ethical and societal expectations represent yet another set of restrictions. All of these constraints, whether explicit or implicit, can critically influence your organization and must be accounted for in your document strategy.

Finding and collecting this information may seem overwhelming. After all, not everyone is privy to upper-management reporting. But with thoughtful investigation and inquiry you will discover much of what you need in published reports. Fill in the blanks by speaking with managers and decision-makers who can describe how these fundamental areas of concern influence your organization.

You can quickly determine a direction for your document strategy by exploring the basic needs, pressures and constraints that drive your business. How can your document strategy assist with these important success measures? Ideas for improvement will come more quickly with a review of these fundamentals. Solutions will become more apparent once your baseline is established. If you do nothing more than

Case Example: XYZ Laboratories

 Consider the case of XYZ laboratories, a fictitious pharmaceutical firm that manufactures over-the-counter drugs. Their Baseline Assessment has uncovered the following data on the left. Viewing these needs, pressures and constraints through the perspective of a document strategy, XYZ asks the questions posed on the right.

Hard Numbers

Realize a 7% growth in annual sales. Keep operating costs below a 4% increase.

Hard Numbers

How can a document strategy help to increase sales and mitigate increases in operating expense? What contributions might documents make to these percentage targets? How can that be demonstrated?

Competitive Pressures

Maintain production quality at less than 1% defect rate. Maintain prices 8% - 10% below market competitors

Competitive Pressures

How can a document strategy assist with quality control and help keep production costs down? How can documents help track defects and eliminate waste?

Operational Pressures

Maintain operations at a high rate of efficiency (approx. 90%) while reducing workforce by 2%. Minimize inefficiencies in workflow between diverse locations (due to merger and acquisition of several competitors in different locations).

Operational Pressures

How are people spending their time with documents? How can documents eliminate redundant or unnecessary work? How can documents help connect the various workgroups within the company and bring people together? How can documents prompt efficient actions and guide workflow.

Constraints, Requirements and Expectations

Gain regulatory approval of four new products.
Comply with federal standards on all products.
Improve the corporate image in the local community.

Constraints, Requirements and Expectations

What role do documents play in the process to gain regulatory approval? How can documents support efforts to comply with standards? How can documents build a positive image of the company?

examine these aspects of your organization you will be well on your way to designing a document strategy that will make a difference.

Step Two: Objectives and Strategies

 Objectives and strategies link corporate performance to the bottom-line. To determine your direction, you must understand how your document strategy can benefit the specific and measurable objectives of your firm.

A better Baseline Assessment might have helped the architects of a European e-commerce venture in 1997. *E-Christmas.com* was designed to sell products from nine European countries online. Several high profile companies sponsored the Web site, yet sales were disappointing. The trouble was that important trade regulations were overlooked.

Import-export restrictions prohibited or impeded sales over national borders. After only a few weeks the Web site was shut down. When asked about the trade rule faux pas, one company official said: "Logistics are crucial, yet often overlooked." [7]

Long-Term Objectives and Grand Strategy

Your firm's long-term objectives are the results it aims to achieve over a multi-year period. These objectives typically focus on areas like profitability, return on investment, competitive position, market leadership, productivity, and customer satisfaction and retention. Your organization's grand strategy is how your firm intends to meet its long-term objectives. This plan indicates how your objectives are to be achieved, when they should be achieved and to what degree they should benefit the company. For your document strategy to have vital and important results, it must facilitate the grand strategy of your firm.

Short-Term Objectives and Operating Strategies.

The results that your organization hopes to see within one year are short-term objectives. While somewhat similar in nature to long-term objectives, the outcomes associated with short-term objectives will be more specific and more immediately measured. Most of the operational and functional strategies in your organization will be set to achieve short-term objectives. The culmination of those achievements should, wherever possible, be a part of the framework of your document strategy.

View these figures with a document strategy in mind. How can a document strategy bring about a positive result for XYZ laboratories? How can a strategy assist with their short-term objectives? How can it help to fulfill their grand strategy? Are there ways that documents might increase customer satisfaction and retention? Can documents assist in revenue growth by boosting sales conversion? Will improvements in document systems reduce operating expenses, bolster on-time performance and facilitate regulatory approval? If the answer is yes, then you are well on your way. Follow these compass points as you map your document strategy.

Step Three: Mission and Vision

It's a long way between the basement and the boardroom. Ironically, the people most likely to be pressed into service to design a document strategy are selected for their technical expertise or their tactical experience, not for their intimate knowledge of corporate

Case Example: XYZ Laboratories

 What are the specific ways your firm tracks the achievement of its objectives? Imagine that these short- and long-term goals and objectives are the measurements that XYZ Laboratories will use to determine how the company is doing.

Customer satisfaction

An index for satisfaction of surveyed customers based on a 10-point scale with 10 being "extremely satisfied."

1999 baseline: 8.1

2000 objective: 9.3

2005 objective: 9.7

Customer retention

Describes the number of lost customers versus new customers based on "zero defect" – one hundred percent new customers, zero percent lost customers.

1999 baseline: 82/18

2000 objective: 91/9

2005 objective: 97/3

Sales conversion on new customers

Describes the number of newly attained customers versus the number of prospective customers.

1999 baseline: 21%

2000 objective: 30%

2005 objective 35%

Revenue growth

A percent indicator of increased or decreased revenue over the prior year.

1998 - 1999 baseline 7.8%

1999 - 2000 objective 10%

2001 – 2005 objective 15%

Operating expense

The percentage of operating expense versus gross revenue.

1999 baseline: 12%

2000 objective: 10.5%

2005 objective: 8.5%

On-time performance – product to market

1999 baseline: 83%

2000 objective: 94%

2005 objective: 100%

Regulatory Licensing

Achievement of license and accreditation by regulatory body.

1999 baseline: 1-year

2000 objective: 5-year

2005 objective: renew 5-year

strategy. Proficiencies with computers, programming and printers, or experience with production and process make them the logical choice. Some have assumed the dubious role of document strategist by default because no one else wants to hassle with documents. Either way, the "back office" role of the document profession rarely cultivates an intimate understanding of the vision that drives business "up front."

By understanding short- and long-term goals, you establish compass points from which to chart the direction of your document strategy.

In an ideal world, everyone is keenly knowledgeable of organizational purpose and direction. Each improvement effort, every departmental objective, and all the functions of day-to-day work are directly aligned with the mission and vision of the company. But we know this is not so. Although they may appear somewhat fluffy or hard to quantify, the mission and vision of your organization are the foundation upon which it develops specific objectives and strategies. For your document strategy to be of lasting benefit it must tap into the most important aspects of your company's mission and serve the vision of executive policy-makers.

"For those with a technological bent, understanding mission and vision may not seem to be particularly inspirational, but it is a valuable exercise because it tells us what we should focus on." says Leslie Smid. "If we have to divide our attention, then our focus should be on those things that are most likely to fulfill our mission and vision. The ultimate question for any strategist, document or otherwise is: Are my efforts aligned with my business and where it's planning to go?"

Mission

You have probably seen your company's mission statement. They are printed everywhere from annual statements to employee paychecks. While some may argue that a mission statement does very little to guide the day-to-day operation

---

Mission Statements

Federal Express: "To produce outstanding financial returns by providing totally reliable, competitively superior global air-ground transportation of high priority goods and documents that require rapid, time-sensitive delivery."

Cadillac Motor Car Company: "To engineer, produce, and market the world's finest automobiles, known for uncompromised levels of distinctiveness, comfort, convenience, and refined performance."

Intel: "Do a great job for our customers, employees and stockholders by being the preeminent building block supplier to the computing industry worldwide."

---

of a business, it can help provide a useful foundation when designing a document strategy.

A mission statement is a proclamation about your organization's driving purpose, philosophy and goals. It might also define your products and services, and describe specific methods or technologies your firm will use to provide those products and services. It might also express the types of markets that are most important, who your core customers are and the internal competencies needed to do business.

Many people working in large organizations today cannot recap the mission of their organization. What is your company's mission statement? When was the last time you read it? How does your document strategy serve the mission of your organization?

Vision

Corporate vision can be narrow or broad. One no-nonsense executive puts it this way: "We want to increase revenue and cut costs...what more of a vision do you want?" Others have more wide-ranging beliefs about the purpose, values and principles that should focus corporate vision. To understand of the vision of your organization may require that you compile a composite of both the formal statements of purpose as well as the more casually implied vision of executives, project sponsors and managers. Interview decision-makers in your organization that are willing to describe their view of the corporate vision. Your task is to understand the unique purpose of your company. What is it that sets your firm apart from other companies? What is unique about your product? What are the particulars of your market and your areas of emphasis?

Many organizations develop vision statements that describe where the organization is headed and what it intends to be. A vision statement depicts a future that would not happen by itself. The statement may articulate the basic characteristics that shape your organization's approach to doing business. Often, it is linked directly to customer needs and conveys a general strategy for achieving the mission.[8]

> **Vision Statements**
>
> *PepsiCo:* "We will be an outstanding company by exceeding customer expectations through empowered people, guided by shared values."
>
> *Alcoa:* "We will be dedicated to excellence through quality, creating value for customers, employees and shareholders through innovation, technology and operational expertise.

"Understanding corporate vision gets people working in the same direction, and a Baseline Assessment serves as a communication tool to be sure your vision is clear," says Debbie Cannon, president of DAC Enterprises. "Corporations are becoming more and more compartmentalized. People make decisions, and although you like to think that they are hooked into the big picture, it's more likely that they are hooked into their own view of things. You need to understand how all the corporate pieces fit together, what the corporate vision is, and where you're headed. From there you can move forward and facilitate that vision." [9]

Carefully and continuously check how your efforts line up with your firm's mission and vision by asking questions like:

- What are the specific initiatives underway to achieve your company's mission and vision?
- Who is ultimately responsible for seeing those initiatives through?
- How can a document strategy help fulfill those initiatives?
- What new initiatives can a document strategy provide that will fulfill your mission and vision?

Develop a Comprehensive View

The essential function of your Baseline Assessment is to make certain that as you develop your document strategy you do so with a relatively comprehensive view of your organization. That comprehensive view includes an understanding of your organization's needs, pressures and constraints, as well as your company's mission and vision. How your mission and vision touch you personally is probably through the impact of your hard numbers and business pressures, but be clear about the links between your document strategy and your business.

You do not need to conduct your Baseline Assessment in any particular order, as long as you make sure to examine all of the pieces. Good decisions are based on good data, and your objective is to get as complete a picture of your organization as you can without going into analysis paralysis. You need enough information to make informed directional decisions and to be able to write your business case in terms that decision-makers will understand and appreciate.

A Baseline Assessment will serve you well if for no other reason than it will help you to get "out of your box." In order to sell your strategy, you must be able to speak the language of the business. If you are going to persuade executives and sponsors, you will need to have a working knowledge of the fundamental business needs, pressures and constraints of your organization. Your understanding of these aspects of your business will be an important leverage to establish credibility, sell your strategy and gain support.

Get Yourself Located

Getting yourself located is a matter of reference. When navigating your document strategy, where you start from has a direct correlation to where you end up. Even the most precise directional planning is only relevant if you have a well-charted baseline as a starting point. Establish that starting point with your Baseline Assessment.

Navigators at sea use latitude and longitude to determine their location and chart their course. The concepts of latitude and longitude have been around since ancient times, but Greek astronomer Ptolemy was the first to document their use when he created the first world atlas in 150 AD. Ptolemy knew that the sun, moon and planets pass almost directly overhead at the Equator. It was because of this natural occurrence that he placed zero-degree latitude at the Equator. Ptolemy was free, however, to place his prime meridian – the zero-degree longitude line – wherever he liked. He chose to run it through the Canary Islands. [10]

Today the prime meridian is located in Greenwich, near London (hence the term *Greenwich Mean Time*). But depending on the mapmaker, it has been located in cities as diverse as: Rome, Copenhagen, Jerusalem, Paris, and even Philadelphia. Finally, in 1851, zero longitude settled in Greenwich, but the placement of the prime meridian throughout history has been purely arbitrary.

Suppose a skipper plots a course "forty degrees west." If he begins his calculations in Philadelphia, not Greenwich, the ship will arrive in a location entirely different than the one where he intended to go.

Questions to Consider:

- What are the hard numbers that measure your company's performance?

- What pressures and constraints influence your firm's daily performance and overall success?

- What are the most important aspects of why your organization exists?

- What are the strategic visions and tactical objectives that guide your organization every day?

- What are the most important initiatives currently underway?

- Where are the most immediate opportunities to solve problems or improve processes?

- In what ways do documents influence all of the above?

4

Documents, Technology and People

The next step in the Document Strategy Model continues your assessment in three specific areas of inquiry: documents, technology and people. These three elements are essentially the "what, how and who" of your document strategy: *what* documents are important, *how* they are produced and *who* cares about how they perform in the process.

Documents are, naturally, the subject of your strategy. They are what you are aiming to improve. In order to increase the strategic value and tactical effectiveness of your documents, it stands to reason that you should determine which ones are the most important to your organization. Using the information you collected in your Baseline Assessment, you will identify a "vital few" documents that offer the highest return and the best likelihood for success in terms of meeting the needs of your organization. You will target these documents in your strategy.

Technology, on the other hand, enables the document process. Computers, printers, databases, networks, and all their associated systems and programs are the means by which documents are created, produced and processed. In this chapter, you will survey the technology used to produce your target documents. Once you have assessed your current capabilities, you will investigate how trends in technology might influence or improve your process. The information you gather will provide the basis for your recommendations regarding equipment purchases, software upgrades and system changes.

Documents

- What are the documents used in your critical business functions?
- Which have the highest potential return on your effort?
- Which have the best probability for success?

Technology

- What are the technologies and processes that produce these documents?
- Are existing capabilities underutilized or overworked?
- What new and developing technology is available that might improve your process?

People

- Who are the people that create, process and care about how your documents perform?
- What are the needs and requirements of this document constituency?
- How well are their needs currently being met?

An old farmers saying once warned, *you can't milk a cow with a two-legged stool*. Documents, technology and people are like three legs of your document strategy. Remove one, or shorten it, and you'll loose balance, stability and perspective.

In the end, people are the reason documents are produced – without cavemen there would be no cave drawings; without people there would be no documents. It seems reasonable, therefore, that the people who populate the document process in your organization are the best people to describe the process. Here, you will examine your *document constituency* with an aim to recognize and incorporate their needs and objectives into the design of your strategy. Authors, readers, producers and stakeholders – all have specific, varied, and sometimes conflicting, interests in your document strategy. You must include these interests when planning specific actions within your strategy.

Quite simply, *documents* are created with *technology* to be used by *people*, so it makes sense that these three factors surface as guiding beacons for your document strategy. Mapping the course of your plans from these perspectives will help direct the latitude of your effort and ensure that your design process is comprehensive yet manageable. As a result, your directional decisions will not only be possible but practical, and more likely to lead you to a more profitable destination.

As noted earlier, however, you should not regard this framework as a linear process. The interaction between documents, technology and people is fluid and will overlap. The design of your strategy will benefit from a similarly fluid approach. As you learn more about your documents you will learn more about the technology used to produce them. As you become familiar with the people who have a stake in your documents, you will begin to understand which documents matter most to your organization. As you learn more about your current capabilities, you will be better able to ascertain how trends in technology might improve your process in the future. So don't get caught up in the exact order of your efforts. Adjust, adapt and apply this framework to your particular situation.

Consider that there may be hundreds, if not thousands, of documents within your organization. Some are more important than others. Some are obsolete while others have a lifetime of importance. Some documents drive vital business functions while others languish in forgotten workflow, living a life of their own because "we've always done it this way." Regardless, documents are everywhere – a persistent element of everyday work. Their sheer numbers and pervasiveness can dampen the spirits of the most enthusiastic document strategist. An organized approach is essential if you hope to get your hands around the scope of your strategy.

In 1997, the State of Wisconsin's Department of Administration found they had over 48,000 administrative forms. This overwhelming number did not include the multitude of other documents used statewide. According to Sandy Kreul, executive assistant administrator of the division of technology management, a strategic approach was the only way to get a handle on the daunting task of reviewing the many forms used throughout their various agencies. "Our ad hoc efforts over the years had, for the most part, failed to address the exponential growth of our forms, redundant data collection and inefficient workflow. A more coordinated effort was needed."

As part of Wisconsin's award-winning strategy, [1] Kreul put a "documents-technology-people" framework into action: "To begin with, we set out to understand the original purpose of each document, how it evolved in our environment and its strategic importance," says Kreul. "From there, we determined whether or not the form was still needed and if it was still effectively serving its purpose. Next, we looked to see if we needed to collect new information, or if the information we had already could be reused and shared in new ways through the use of new or different technology. Ultimately, the concerns of the people who use each document drove the final recommendations." [2]

Wisconsin's document strategy saved the state nearly $3 million initially, with an anticipated continued annual savings of $1.2 million.

Technology is also pervasive and complex. Depending on your company, document processing can involve everything from legacy mainframe systems to the latest Web-enabled solution. Your documents may mutate between paper and digital incarnations in seemingly random and incomprehensible ways. To make informed decisions and valuable recommendations, you must understand your current technology as well as the range of possibilities presented by new and developing technology.

People play the biggest and most varied role in the document process. As such, they should be featured prominently within the design of your strategy. The population of your document constituency – authors, producers, stakeholders and readers – can be significant. Authors and readers have specific needs that each document must fulfill. Technicians, printer operators and programmers – the people who produce your documents – have an entirely different set of requirements and constraints. Stakeholders, including executives, regulators and investors, also have an important stake in the performance of your documents.

Documents

 The number of documents found within an organization can be so overwhelming that it paralyzes attempts to design and implement a document strategy. While there may be thousands of documents in your organization, the central question is: What are the documents that drive the essential functions of your organization? Chances are good that only a few documents are absolutely indispensable to your business. You don't necessarily need to re-engineer *every* document. Start your strategy with only the most essential.

The Pareto Principle

Joseph Juran, a venerable leader of the Total Quality Management movement, coined the concept of the "Pareto Principle" in the 1950s after he observed that the majority of problems result from only a few causes. Juran named the rule after Vilfredo Pareto, a 19th century Italian economist, who

Case Example: XYZ Laboratories

Suppose XYZ Laboratories has approximately fifty thousand documents that are used within their enterprise. In order to determine which documents are most important, a team of managers, technicians and production personnel conduct an assessment. They frame their investigation using the following functional categories, and then assess the number of documents that are used within each business function.

Total Documents	50,000	100%

Core Functions	Number of Core Documents	
Marketing	2,500	
Finance	2,000	
Research	3,200	
Production	800	
Human Resources	1,500	
Total Core Documents	10,000	20%

As a result, XYZ determines that only twenty percent of the total number of documents found company-wide actually drives the core functions of their business. Only ten thousand of the original fifty thousand are "core documents." The rest are found to have only periodic or specialized importance, or are used in secondary functions that are nonessential. Many documents are found to be obsolete, duplicate or redundant.

Ten thousand is still a daunting number, however, so XYZ takes the next step by asking: Of this twenty percent, which documents are absolutely essential for our business to run? Which have the capacity to bring business to its knees? If ranked in priority, which documents rise to the top?

Core Functions	Mission-Critical Documents
Marketing	475
Finance	300
Research	575
Production	350
Human Resources	300
Mission-Critical Documents	2,000

The surviving two thousand documents are seen as "mission-critical" for XYZ Laboratories. Out of ten thousand core documents, only twenty percent remain.

determined that eighty percent of the wealth in Milan was owned by only twenty percent of the people. Some people refer to this idea as the "80-20 rule." Juran first applied the notion in a practical sense by suggesting that poor quality can often be successfully addressed by attacking the few major causes that result in most of the problems.[3] In much the same way, identifying the "vital few" documents within your organization will direct your attention to those documents that are the most important and ensure a more fruitful return on your effort.

Target Documents – the "Vital Few"

Once you have determined which documents are the most important for your business to run, you still need a place to start. As Juran might suggest, it is important to identify those "vital few" documents that provide the most potential benefit in terms of improving the performance of your organization. If you could select only a handful of documents to target in your strategy, which ones would they be?

Select your target documents by returning to your Baseline Assessment. Which documents have the greatest influence on the success of your organization? Which ones play a part in realizing your firm's objectives and vision? Which are in most need of improvement, are the most troublesome, or provide the most potential return for your effort?

"You have to pick what you are going to champion as reasonable elements of a document strategy," says Mark Wahl, executive administrator of the division of technology management for the State of Wisconsin. "If you pick something that is clearly unreasonable, then you'll set yourself up for failure. So what I tried to do was pick the most significant documents, and ones that I felt would be successful. Those are the efforts I would champion."[4]

The XYZ example illustrates how you can reduce the seemingly overwhelming scope of your document strategy to a more manageable project by concentrating only on those documents that are vitally important. You may find that there are several, or only a few, that are absolutely essential for your business to run. XYZ has elected to concentrate on these "Top-Ten"

Case Example: XYZ Laboratories

 The team at XYZ uses their Baseline Assessment to design the criteria needed to select their "vital few" target documents from the remaining two thousand. They ask the following questions:

- Which documents have the biggest influence on our numbers and measures?

- Which help manage the needs, pressures and constraints of doing business?

- Which contribute to meeting our specific goals and objectives?

- Which serve our overall mission and vision?

- Which are the most troublesome in terms of support, errors and efficiency?

- Which are the most costly to create, produce and process?

- Which have the biggest influence on customer satisfaction?

- Which have the biggest influence on efficiency?

- Which serve important strategic initiatives?

The answers help XYZ pair down their two thousand mission-critical documents to a short list of the most vital documents. One manager equates this process with *Late Night with David Letterman*. "What is your 'Top-Ten' list?' – The most essential with the most potential?"

While they agree that there are other documents that also need attention, the team at XYZ finalizes their "Top-Ten" list this way:

Core Functions	Target Documents
Marketing	New product literature
	Customer letters
Finance	Monthly customer statements
	Large account billings
Research	Patent research reports
	Regulatory compliance documentation
Production	Work request tracking reports
	Inventory and production reports
Human Resources	Employee benefits reports
	Hiring and termination forms

Number of Target Documents 10

rather than attempt to re-engineer all fifty thousand documents within their enterprise. After their work with this batch is completed, they will select another group of documents and continue their strategic efforts.

During your assessment, you will likely find a number of documents that are redundant, obsolete or out-of-date. As mentioned in Chapter One, if a document is not part of the solution, it's probably part of the problem. Now is a good time to identify those documents that are no longer useful and consider eliminating them.

Technology

 Now that you have selected your target documents, your next step is to examine the technology used to create, produce and process those documents. What are the requirements of the process? How do things get done, and why? What are the strengths and weaknesses of your current technology? Your aim is to get a brief, yet comprehensive view of your current capabilities without becoming caught in analysis paralysis. While the scope of your assessment may cover a wide range of technology – everything from web presses to Web pages can be part of your document processing environment – the key is to avoid becoming sidetracked from your purpose by an overdose of technical jargon and marketing rhetoric. Concentrate on your target documents and examine the technology used to produce your "Top-Ten."

Document Life Cycle

One way to approach this assessment is to follow your target documents through their life cycle. While the life cycle of a document can be described in various ways, assume your documents have these phases in common:

Creation: Assembling information into a purposeful design.

Production: Presenting and delivering a document on paper or in digital form.

Revision: Reusing or updating a document, or parts of it, for an assortment of reasons.

Archive: Storing a document for later retrieval.

Retirement: A document is deemed obsolete and is destroyed or deleted, or perhaps simply forgotten for good.

The Document Life Cycle

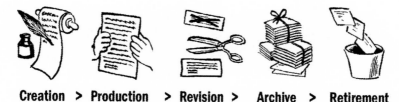

Creation > Production > Revision > Archive > Retirement

Follow each of your target documents through this life cycle. What are the technological aspects and requirements of the process?

Creation

Where does the information come from that populates the document?

- What databases are used?
- Which data files contribute to the document?
- How is variable and static information used?
- Does the information reside on a mainframe? A server? A disk?

How is the format designed?

- What layout software is used?
- Are templates or overlays used?
- How are text and graphic elements put together?

Production

How is the document produced, processed and presented?

- Is the document issued on paper? On screen? On disk? On the Web? To a hand-held device? All of the above?
- What software and hardware is used in the process?
- What protocols, programs and languages facilitate production?
- Does the document exist in multiple formats (e.g., paper and digital) or multiple languages?
- Is equipment overworked or underutilized?
- Are there seasonal fluctuations that impact production (e.g., tax season, year end, etc.)?

Revision

How are revisions to the document achieved?

- Are revisions handled the same way as the original creation?
- Are the original authors revising the document, or someone else?
- When revisions are made, what happens to the original version? How are revisions tracked and monitored?
- Does the document get revised and repurposed for other uses?

Archive

How is the document saved and archived?

- In what format is the document archived (e.g., paper or digital)?
- What software and hardware is used to store and access it?

- What protocols, programs and languages are used?

- When retrieved, will the document resume its prior format or be used in different ways?

- Are there legal ramifications for the archived document?

Retirement

Once the document reaches the end of its useful life, how is the document retired?

- Is the document retained in an archive or eliminated?

- What software and hardware is used?

- Will pieces of the original document live on in other incarnations?

Adapt this process to fit your particular situation. Remove questions that do not apply and add questions of your own and from your co-workers. Remember to concentrate only on your most vital and important documents – your Top Ten. *Your aim is to bring together a profile that reflects how these few documents are created and processed.* This will help keep things manageable and organized. If you are already tech-savvy, this assessment will serve as a way to organize the details of your hardware, software and systems. If your technological experience is far from guru status, building this profile will be an important step toward managing your project and understanding your technology. In any event, reviewing the technology used to produce your target documents is a valuable exercise that will help you gauge the strengths and weaknesses of your current capabilities and judge the potential benefits of new and developing technology.

Investigate New and Developing Technology

With your assessment of your current technology completed, you are now in a good position to assess how trends in technology may be of potential benefit in the future. This may require that you look "outside the box" of what you are familiar and comfortable with. Ask questions like:

- Can we do things differently?
- What are the "best practices" in the industry?
- Who is successful using what technology?
- Do new trends have potential in your environment?
- What technologies will enhance your current systems?
- What technologies should take the place of systems that you know have to be replaced?

Designing a document strategy requires that you be familiar with the variety of technological options available to you. You will need to understand how trends in technology can be translated into measurable and meaningful improvement for your particular organization. Deciphering these developments will require more than attending an occasional trade show or marketing presentation. A consistent and dedicated effort is needed. "Into each era of business new technologies are thrust," says industry pundit P.C. McGrew. "If your strategy is ill conceived with regard to changing technologies, your plans will be buried within a year." [5]

One way to become familiar with developing technology is to canvas the industry for new and different approaches. Your aim is to uncover options that have potential in your environment. Look for trends that set the stage for future innovation and industry direction. Seek out the stories of success and failure of other organizations that have adopted new technology. Search for vendors and consultants that appear to be keeping pace with changes in technology. This can be done in a variety of ways, all of which require that you be proactive, curious and creative.

- Attend industry conferences and trade shows. If you cannot attend, at least get the information from the events you miss. Often, information highlighting the event is released on a Web site or CD.
- Attend local association chapter meetings and user groups.
- Read industry trade journals and magazines.

- Consult with your current vendors as well as vendors that you have not used.

- Visit other facilities and organizations to determine what "best practices" may benefit your organization.

- Examine unrelated but similar production processes (e.g., manufacturing, etc).

- Attend seminars, college courses or technical training.

- Engage an outside consultant.

- Join industry associations and seek ideas and advice from other industry professionals. Attend seminars, meetings and training sessions.

- Search the Internet, the Web and newsgroups. Subscribe to online newsletters and industry "list-serve" e-mail services.

- Search academic databases and related FTP servers.

The development curve of new technology is double-edged. On one hand, innovation provides a seemingly endless selection of solutions to choose from. On the other hand, finding the right technology for your particular situation may not be as easy as walking an exhibit floor. And technological change comes at such a rapid pace that it is hard to keep up. What was not possible only a few short months ago may be commonplace today. Capabilities you would not have considered as important initially may suddenly become essential requirements of your new strategy.

At this point in your strategy design, it is important to avoid giving in to the temptation to jump ahead to solutions – a particularly enticing tendency when technology is involved. Continue to collect information and build your perspective. You will find that the best directions become clear as you begin to bring "the big picture" into focus.

One more word of caution is needed. If you introduce new or different technology into your process, be careful not to disturb what is working well. Nearly every process has some features that are worth keeping. Any technology you consider will likely have both positive and negative implications for whatever your current process is. You should be careful to accurately assess how your process is currently working, and why, before you sign the purchase order. [6] "Sound business strategies will survive. Technology-bound product implementations may not," says Dick Quinn, from the University of Central Florida's College of Business Administration. "If the process of building a document strategy is viewed only as a collection of products, the corporate view of document strategies (as ineffective or frivolous) will never change." [7]

The Impact of the Internet

It is impossible to discuss technology and how it influences the design of your document strategy without mentioning the impact of the Internet. The Internet is touted as technology that will change our lives – and that may be true – but the implications of how the Internet will affect our business climate and influence the way people communicate is beyond the scope of this book. One essential question remains, however: What role should the Internet have in your document strategy? The answer is: It depends.

The potential role of the Internet in your strategy depends on the needs and objectives of your particular organization. Again, return to your Baseline Assessment for guidance. Many organizations expect the Internet to help them save money by reducing printing and mailing costs. Others feel that marketing communications, e-commerce and customer contacts are the top benefits of the Internet. Some view access to the vast amounts of information available on the Internet as the most valuable way they can take advantage of being wired. None of this comes to pass without substantial cost in terms of money, effort and time. Rely on your Baseline Assessment to bring to light your most important organizational objectives. Then determine if, or how, the Internet will serve those objectives.

Whatever the impact to your organization, it is likely that the Internet will play some kind of role in your document strategy. Nearly all companies have a Web site and about half are using it to conduct business. Almost without exception, corporations believe that the Internet will help them sell more product, reach more customers and share information more easily and dynamically. [8]

"The Internet has changed our model, " says Toby Cobrin, from Xplor International. "It's a technology that obviously drives cultural change, but most importantly, it has changed the way we interface with information. It has accelerated the timing of things by providing instantaneous access to information. As a result, even traditional information delivery methods will be required to respond with more quickness and versatility. The Internet might not be the panacea that everyone thinks it should be, but it is definitely changing the way we deal with information." [9]

How can the Internet:

- Influence your hard numbers, mitigate pressures and ease operating constraints?

- Improve the measurements that indicate company performance?

- Mitigate the problems and meet the needs of doing business every day?

- Help to achieve short- and long-term objectives and strategies?

- Improve customer service, process workflow, and operational efficiency?

- Serve specific strategies and initiatives, and fulfill the mission and vision of the organization?

"The future is a big place, and the Internet may or may not play a role in your strategy," says P.C. McGrew. "However, if you go the route of the Internet as an information delivery medium, there is no doubt that a serious, well-refined strategy is required to ensure that both traditional and Web-based documents deliver the same types of tangible benefit for your enterprise."

People

 The people who create, use and care about your documents are the best people to provide the finer points of navigation within your strategy. Who can better

describe which documents are important, how they are used, how they perform and how things could be better? Documents are the one single thing that can stop business cold yet no one is in charge. But for any document it is possible to identify a *document constituency* – the people who influence the document process: authors, producers, stakeholders and readers. Collectively, these people are in charge.

You must identify the people who compose the constituency of each of your target documents. Each member has an important involvement with your document process, so their needs, difficulties, constraints and requirements are important directional pointers for your strategy. Furthermore, your constituents have a personal stake in how each document performs and will likely be the targets of whatever changes you propose. You will need their support and cooperation if you hope to succeed.

"The fact is that a great many people need to work together to get this thing off the ground, let alone land it safely," says document design expert Dr. Michael Turton. "Their paths may not have crossed thus far, but each will certainly approach the subject from different angles and their objectives will be different, possibly conflicting with those of others." Turton suggests that understanding who to get involved in strategy design, *before* any decisions are made, is the "single most important aspect of the whole document strategy process." [10]

The Document Constituency

The people who make up your document constituency are the people who use your documents, have responsibility for their existence and have a stake in how well they perform. Chances are, you have already made contact with many of the people who make up your document constituency. Your assessments and investigations thus far have already introduced you to people who care about and have a stake in how your documents perform. But there may be other people whose membership in your document constituency is not immediately apparent. As you learn more about target documents and the technology used to produce them, the members of your document constituency become easier to spot. Some of the people will come easily to mind because they have already accepted ownership of a document or have a long history managing part of the process. Others may be less ready to accept accountability or are simply unaware that they have anything to do with a "document process." Nonetheless, the people who create, produce and care about your documents will have, at different times, differing concerns, goals and interests. Your aim is to search out these people and include their needs and concerns in the design of your strategy.

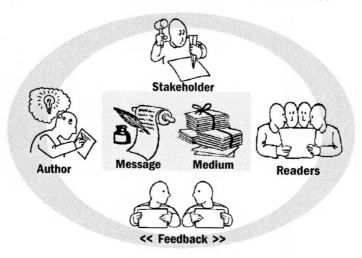

The Document Constituency Model

You can identify members of your document constituency by using these four categories:

Authors	the writers, composers and content providers, both intentional and implied.
Producers	the creators, producers and processors of your documents.
Stakeholders	the people who have a stake in your documents performance.
Readers	the people who use, read, and react to your documents.

Each of these people has a different set of needs, expectations and constraints. *Authors* have specific objectives about a document's content, for example, that may, or may not, coincide with the needs and expectations of the *reader*.

Producers have pressures and constraints that must often be overcome in order to meet the expectations of *stakeholders* who have a broader interest in how documents communicate and carry on business.

In addition, the activities and requirements of the people within your constituency will influence and determine both the *message* of your documents and the *medium* used to deliver them. Document attributes – what a document says, the information it contains, its format and construction, and whether it is presented on paper or in digital form – are entirely determined by the people in your document constituency.

Authors

 A document author is the person or persons who are concerned about what a document says and how readers will react. An author could be an individual, a team or an entire department. Corporate documents often contain information from various sources and are authored by several different departments who may, or may not, be working in concert. These multiple authors may not even be aware of each other's presence in the process (one certain indicator that a document strategy is needed).

Identifying a single document author may not always be possible in a large organization. While there may be some documents that are written, designed and published by a single person who is solely responsible for their content, media and performance, it is more likely that several authors are involved. Regardless, each has a common objective to convert information into action and to ensure that the right message is effectively communicated to a reader.

Producers

Document producers are the individuals, work groups or departments who provide the "output" of your document systems. They are the people who are responsible for production of your target documents – everyone from artists, typesetters and system programmers, to printer operators, mail clerks and Web masters.

It is essentially impossible to meet the needs of the other members of your document constituency if the needs of your producers are not met. Producers need the right information from the right sources at the right time, as well as the right staffing and equipment in order to produce documents with acceptable quality, timeliness and cost. Document producers often feel the pinch between meeting the needs of their customers and working within operating constraints. As a result, their needs are often at odds with the needs of the other members of your document constituency. A key objective of your document strategy should be to understand and reduce this gap.

"Corporate culture often contains a weird prejudice against the people who actually *produce* things," says author and Web consultant Paul Telles. "It often seems that the big thinkers are regarded as the real soul of the company. Without a clear means of production and the expertise to run them, however, the greatest ideas will fail to bear fruit." [11]

Stakeholders

 Stakeholders are customers of document performance. They are concerned with both the strategic and tactical aspects of your target documents: how well they convert information into action and how cost effectively and efficiently they can be produced.

Stakeholders might include marketing executives concerned about whether consumers will purchase a product, financial officers concerned about how quickly they will pay, or divisional vice presidents concerned about the costs involved with document production. Other stakeholders might include government regulators, internal auditors or corporate legal counsel who are concerned with document security, content and verbiage. Suppliers are stakeholders too, since they supply the materials, machinery and technology that make your document process run.

Stakeholders can have a significant influence on both the contents of a document and the medium used to present it. Both authors and producers take their cue from stakeholders when it comes to what and how documents communicate. As a result, the needs and constraints of authors and producers can change depending on the needs and constraints of stakeholders.

Readers

Readers are the audience of your documents. They are the people who react and respond to the information contained in your target documents. Reader reaction is the litmus test of document performance, so how information is converted into action is high on the list of concerns for both authors and stakeholders. As a result, the expectations and requirements of readers are important to your strategy. The integrity of information contained in a document, its timely arrival, and how clearly it communicates are some important criteria for all readers. Privacy, security and accuracy are important to readers outside your company, while readers inside your organization may be primarily concerned with how easy documents are to use, find and file.

Readers also influence both the message and the medium of your documents. If the reader of your target document is a pharmacist, for example, the content you provide may need to be detailed, and the message may need to be meticulous and specific. On the other hand, if your document is targeted at senior citizens that get prescriptions filled, your document may need to be less technical and easier to understand – even the font size may be an important factor. And while a pharmacist may be happy to refer to the Internet for up-to-date information, Medicare recipients are less likely to surf the Web for the latest on prescription drugs.

The needs, constraints and requirements of your document constituency will guide the decisions and actions within your document strategy. Additionally, by consulting these people during the design of your strategy, you will be more likely to have their support and participation in whatever changes you propose. Ultimately, by identifying your document constituency and understanding their respective needs and constraints, you will be more likely to construct meaningful and effective tactics within your strategy.

Case Example: XYZ Laboratories

XYZ Laboratories has assembled a list of target documents and sets forth to identify a document constituency for each. Below is the constituency identified for XYZ's customer statements, a document identified as vital to their business but often troublesome to produce.

They begin by asking: Who creates this document, who touches it, who uses it, and who cares about its performance? From there, they segment their document constituents into authors, producers, stakeholders and readers. Note that departments as well as specific people are identified as document constituents.

AUTHORS

Information Services:	Cathy Hiatt – Programmer
Finance:	Debbie Faunce – Accounts Payable
Customer Services:	Lynette Cranford – Administrative Specialist
Marketing: Representative	Anthony Zel – Regional Product

PRODUCERS

Information Services:	Kevin Rogers – Corporate Forms Analyst
	Sandra Strait – Print Shop Supervisor
Administrative Services:	Roland Reiniger – Mail Services Supervisor

STAKEHOLDERS

Customer Services:	Cindy Johnson – Manager
Information Services:	Tammy Rivas – Manager
Finance: Payable	Brandon Woods – Manager, Accounts
Marketing:	Lisa Magnuson – Regional Manager

Readers

XYZ Internal Personnel:	Shawn Rosen – Accounts Receivable
External Customers (various):	
	Billing Clerks / Accounts Payable
	Department Secretaries
	Shipping and Receiving Clerks
	Purchasing staff
	Departmental Managers

Constituency Discord

One opportunity for improvement that often lies waiting for a document strategist is *constituency discord.* This is the instance where the needs or objectives of one member or members of your document constituency are at odds with the needs and objectives of other members. Bringing harmony to this discord is one way to find success with your strategy.

For example, suppose two members of your document constituency are Jane Jones and Steve Smith. Jones is a product marketing manager and a document author. Smith is an operations manager and a document producer. Jones is responsible for the content as well as the format and appearance of an important target document. Smith is responsible for producing the finished document and ensuring that it is processed with the most efficient use of labor and equipment. Jones's objective is to increase revenue while Smith's is to reduce operating costs. While both are admirable goals, these seemingly opposing objectives can create discord. As an author, Jones may complain that Smith is unable or unwilling to spend the time and expense to produce a document that serves her objectives. On the other hand, Smith may complain that Jones's objectives are unreasonable and that she does not take into consideration his constraints concerning equipment, cost and workload. How can your document strategy bring harmony to this discord?

Raising Awareness

The key objective of your efforts thus far is to raise your awareness. Consider the adage: *I am able to control only that which I am aware of.* By following the steps described in Chapters Three and Four you will be more aware of "where you are and where you need to go" – the essential perspectives needed to direct the course of your strategy. Build these perspectives by focusing on the baseline needs of your organization, concentrating on your most important documents, and constructing a clear profile of the technology used to produce your documents and the people who care about their performance.

Questions to Consider:

- Which target documents are most important to your organization?"

- What technology is used to produce them?

- What are the technological requirements of the process?

- What new and developing technology is available that might improve the current process?

- Who are the authors, producers, readers and stakeholders of your critical documents?

- What are the requirements of this "document constituency?"

5

Problems and Solutions

A t this point you should have a better idea of "where you are and where you need to go." The question now becomes: How exactly will you get there? No matter how clearly you map your destination, the key to arriving is to chart and execute specific ways to proceed. What actions will you include in your strategy? What problems will you solve, what recommendations will you make and what improvements will you seek? As you navigate your course of action, how will you know where to turn and when you have arrived? This element of the Document Strategy Model defines the route you will take.

As a whole, a document strategy is simply a planned combination of activities with a desired outcome. You must do two things to determine the actions and recommendations that will constitute your strategy:

Identify Problems. What problems exist in the performance of your target documents? What are the gaps between the objectives of your organization, the needs of your document constituency and the performance of your document process? How do these problems prevent you from being successful, and why do they exist? When you clearly identify the problems in your document process, it is easier to be clear about the solutions that you need to solve those problems. If the number of problems you uncover discourages you, be encouraged by the fact that these problems are really opportunities to make a meaningful impact with your document strategy.

Identify Solutions. How will you navigate from your current location to your desired destination? In the end, the solutions you choose embody the strategic direction of your plan. It is important to thoughtfully select the solutions you take on board and judiciously settle on recommendations that make the most sense for your situation.

The following is a four-step process to help you identify problems and solutions:

1. Create a document flow chart.
2. Evaluate the process.
3. Define problems and determine causes.
4. Select solutions and plan specific actions.

A *document flow chart* shows the path a document travels throughout your organization (and beyond). From data to delivery, each of your target documents has a specific and specialized flow. Along the way, various people react and perform in various ways as a result of receiving, reading and using each document. At the same time, a variety of technologies, systems and facilities are engaged to create, produce and deliver each document. A flow chart provides a diagram of the process and is a useful way to examine the performance of each of your target documents.

Once your document flow is charted you must then *evaluate the process*. In this step you appraise how things stack up by developing a set of expectations and key results that are required for each of your target documents. What specific results are needed at each step in the document flow? How must technology and production systems perform in terms of expense, time and effort? How should people react upon receiving your document?

Next, you must *define the problems* that you uncover and *determine the causes*. Only after the problems and deficiencies of the process are clearly defined can you accurately determine their cause. In this step you will compose a problem statement that spells out how each problem affects your organization in specific and measurable terms. From there, you will use a Cause-Effect or *fishbone* diagram to determine why each problem exists and pinpoint the underlying cause(s).

With problems defined and causes determined, you are ready to *select solutions* and plan specific actions for your strategy. This step presents a bit of a quandary, however. With the ever-expanding array of technology and methodology available, how do you know which potential solution is the right one for you? You will overcome this dilemma by using a Paired-Choice Matrix to collect and evaluate ideas and then choose the best solution from a list of several possibilities.

Throughout this process, you should recall that your document strategy has "two wings" – a strategic wing and a tactical wing. By using these perspectives to set your expectations and develop measures to evaluate your process, you will not only improve the tactical facets of your documents (e.g., cutting costs, reducing effort and maximizing investment) but also the strategic aspects as well (i.e., converting information into beneficial action). Your strategy will have broader benefit if you attain a balance between the strategic and tactical wings of your strategy.

Stay the Course

It is tempting to skip all of the prior steps of analysis and evaluation presented thus far in this book and jump right to the "select solutions" phase. Most people want to dive right in and start fixing things, even if they are not sure exactly what is broken or why. At this point *it is imperative that you stay your course*. Consider that the solutions you choose and the actions you take *are* your strategy. The choices you make must be made with a high degree of *informed creativity*. Jumping to conclusions about solutions may seem creative, but if you are not well informed your actions will be ineffective. Even the most creative solution is likely to miss the mark.

Be heartened by the fact that you will now begin to see results from all of your hard work. You will finally find practical uses for the information collected in your Baseline Assessment. You will find value in the perspectives you attained by using documents, technology and people as an investigative framework. Eager executives and sponsors will begin to see results as well. Your analysis and evaluation will repay their patience by providing an essential view point from which to spot profitable ports of call.

To Team or Not to Team...

 At this point, you must ponder one of the great quandaries of strategy development – to team or not to team. A team composed of authors, readers, producers and stakeholders may serve you well when designing a document strategy. Their participation will provide you with important and workable concepts. Team participation also encourages others to support your strategy and pulls together ideas based on real-world experience. Input from individuals who represent various departments and functional areas within your organization will help ensure that your plans will work across your organization and benefit everyone involved. It is for these reasons that Chapter Four stressed the need for you to know your document constituency. A team is an extremely useful tool to gather information and build perspective.

Team decision-making, however, has a down side: It can take longer to get things done. This can be a hindrance for your document strategy when you must seize support and opportunity *now*. Many times, team-based projects drag along slowly over months and garner relatively little productive result. Hours are spent simply arranging meeting rooms, juggling schedules and drafting meeting minutes. Days are spent debating details and haggling over minor points of contention. Weeks go by while team members struggle to balance their "real job" with the additional duties and assignments associated with the project. "Despite popular theory, I'm not a big fan of team decision-making," says Dale Chrystie, vice president of customer support for American Freightways. "Teams are great for gathering information and increasing employee buy-in, but for the most part, the best decisions are ultimately made by an informed autocrat." [1]

According to Leslie Smid, who facilitates a variety of team activities at IBM, the success of team decision-making depends in large degree upon who is guiding the process. "It takes a good facilitator to avoid the traps that teams often fall into," says Smid. "A team leader must drive the decision process so that things don't become cumbersome and confused, yet leave room for conversation and creativity. It is important to strike that balance so that decisions don't just get driven through without getting people's buy-in." [2]

The debate over the value and effectiveness of team decision-making is beyond the scope of this book, but the fact remains that making decisions and recommendations can be more difficult using a team. "In my experience, team decisions rarely differ much from trusting my instincts," says Chrystie. "The main difference between decisions made by a team and those made by a truly knowledgeable manager is that team decisions require more time, effort and expense."

If you choose to use a team to design your strategy, do not cut corners in your assessment and evaluation in order to save time. You will save more time in the long run by asking questions like these now:

- Will your team be part of the decision-making process or used only for information gathering?

- Must team consensus drive decisions or will you, the strategy designer, have the ultimate responsibility of deciding on the final actions and recommendations of your plan?

- How will you walk the line between autocratic and democratic decision-making?

Whatever your approach, be clear about your expectations with team members. "Offer truth in advertising," says Smid. "If folks are clear about their role in the process, it's more likely that they'll give you the information and support you need."

Create a Document Flow Chart

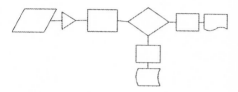 One secret to the success of your document strategy is to spend the time to step back and examine your target documents from a systemic point of view. Unless you understand the overall process you will not be able to determine how to improve it. Achieve this overview by creating a flow chart that follows each target document through your organization and, if necessary, beyond the walls of your company. Identify the steps along the way and the major tasks, actions and events associated with each step. This will lead you to more informed conclusions and beneficial actions for your strategy.

Creating a flow chart is a remarkably clear way to understand all the elements involved in your process. This holistic perspective is important because, for the most part, people are forced to focus their efforts on the day-to-day demands associated with document processing. Managers, supervisors, operators and technicians are often too busy putting out fires to find much time or enthusiasm to attend to an overall document strategy. Everyone is busy attending to their particular part of the process. As a result, it is easy to overlook the larger environment in favor of adopting a quick fix or two.

Chart the Flow

Select a document from your list of target documents and build a flow chart using the symbols above. You may choose to diagram the "easiest" of your target documents first, or you could start with the document that has the most obvious problems. An important project, a particularly demanding customer, or an executive mandate may lead you to concentrate on a particular document. Otherwise, determining where to

Elements of a Flow Chart

Some of the common symbols used in a flow chart are listed below. Elongated circles mark the beginning and ending points of the process. Boxes are used to represent various steps along the way and might include information about the function being performed, the technology used in the function and/or the people receiving the document. Decision points are marked with diamonds that contain yes or no questions. The flow of your document is directed either left or right depending on the answer. Arrows denote document flow, and zigzag arrows indicate an electronic transfer of data.

The symbols you use for your flow chart are not as important as ultimately understanding and documenting the flow. Some people find that small yellow "stickys" are handy when developing a chart. The little squares are convenient because you can move them around and scribble notes on them. (Tip: Turn them sideways to make a diamond.) Adjusting the flow and adding or changing information is quick and easy. Another way to craft a flow chart is simply to use a large piece of paper, a pencil and a big eraser. For many people an uncomplicated low-tech approach is best. If you choose, you can enter the information into a more sophisticated software program once you have developed a clear picture of all the attributes of your document flow.

Symbol	Name	Explanation
⬭	Elongated Circle	Shows the beginning and ending points of a flow chart.
⬜	Box	Represents the steps in your document workflow.

Include a short description of the task performed, the function served, or the person or department who receives your document.

Symbol	Name	Explanation
◇	Diamond	Indicates any decision point.

Include a question that can be answered *yes* or *no*. The direction your document will flow depends on the answer.

Symbol	Name	Explanation
→	Straight Arrow	Shows direction of document flow.

Symbol	Name	Explanation
⌐↘	Zigzag Arrow	Shows an electronic data transfer.

begin may be as easy as following your instincts. At this point, you should have a fairly good sense of which of your documents are the most promising.

Arrange the symbols of your flow chart so that they accurately illustrate the steps in your document's journey. Identify the major tasks that are dependent on your document. Indicate the equipment and technologies used at each point in the flow. Make note of the people or departments that receive, read and use each document. Ask questions such as:

- To what points does your document travel?

- What are the major tasks that are dependent on your document?

- What equipment and technology is used at each major step?

- Is your document "translated" from one "language" to another?

- Which departments use your document and how is information converted into action?

- Does your document travel outside your organization?

- Which decisions link documents with people?

- What functions require technology and people to interact effectively?

This is by no means a comprehensive list of questions, but it will serve to start you thinking about the flow of your target documents and their role in the business processes of your organization. Add questions that have meaning for your particular situation.

Boundaries of a Flow Chart

When charting document flow, especially in a large organization, you could wind up with a flow chart that covers the walls of a small conference room. Working with a diagram that resembles a schematic for the space shuttle is intimidating, so keep your flow chart as simple as possible. Too much detail defeats your purpose. If your flow chart is big enough to wrap

Case Example: XYZ Laboratories

XYZ Laboratories selects their monthly customer billing statements from their list of target documents. The process is represented by the flow chart below, which shows the flow of a billing statement from the time that monthly customer data is generated until the statements are printed and routed to the mailroom.

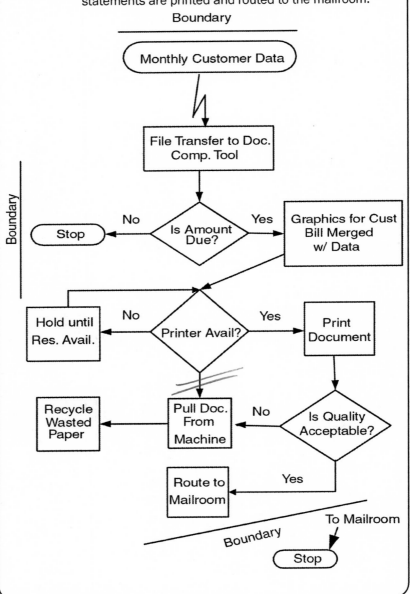

Along the way, decisions shape the document flow, the efforts required and the timeliness of document delivery. In this example, the first question asks: *Is an amount due...yes or no?* If the answer is yes, the process of creating and producing the billing statement continues. If the answer is no, the flow chart comes to a stop. This is because XYZ has chosen to set a boundary at this point in the flow. They have elected not to investigate the process that follows the boundary and will leave that study for another time.

As the flow chart continues, customer data and graphics are merged into a final document. The document is then scheduled for production and delivery. Decisions about printer availability and document quality are made, and eventually the document is printed and routed to the mailroom. Notice that another boundary is placed at this point. XYZ has chosen to stop here for now and plans to launch a more comprehensive investigation of the overall mailing process soon. This examination will involve another flow chart and the two will be linked together later on.

This demonstrates how a document's flow will connect other distinct but related business processes. Charting the flow of your target documents will also point out other important or troubling aspects that did not seem to be significant at first. You may recognize that improvement opportunities are being overlooked in other parts of your process. For example, how is XYZ customer information collected during the month? What documents are used to collect the billing data? What does that part of the flow look like?

This example is fairly limited in scope and intended only to provide a brief illustration of a document flow chart. As you might imagine, a more complicated document flow that encompasses broader boundaries will take time and effort to put together. You must decide how much detail you will attempt to show in your flow chart as well as how far you will extend the limits of your investigation.

around an entire room it is likely that important aspects will get lost in all that detail.

One way to keep your flow chart manageable is to set boundaries for what you will examine. An effective tip is to look at only a portion of the overall flow – from customer service to order processing, for example. This will allow you to focus your attention on a key part of the internal process. On the other hand, you might choose to look at the flow of your document *after* it leaves your organization by examining the process from the point your document leaves your company to when it is received, read and acted upon by an external customer.

Find the Mess

Creating a flow chart is important because it will help you identify the "mess" in your system. A *mess* can be defined as any combination of conditions that produces dissatisfaction. Others might simply say that things are messed-up. Either way, if your document process creates dissatisfaction you need to find the mess and clean it up.

Messes happen because of several conditions:[3]

A lack of knowledge about how the process works. This is particularly troublesome if various people and departments throughout your organization perform the process.

A lack of knowledge about how the process *should* work. Often, the people involved with your documents are unaware of the interrelationships in the flow. Most often, they see their piece in isolation from the big picture.

Lack of attention. Consider the trusted axiom: *You can improve only what you observe.* How can you clean up a mess if you don't know that it exists?

Waste and complexity are overlooked. In the rush to do "more with less," it is ironic that wasted effort and materials are often the result. In the haste to implement new or upgraded technology, complex and unnecessary steps are often allowed to become a norm of the new workflow. You will be tempted to overlook these problems until later, but the result is an inefficient process that eventually becomes a messy legacy.

Excess variation. It is not uncommon for document systems to have been developed and deployed with little regard to how they must operate together. Do you have a mess of different hardware, software and systems in your company? Excess variation an invitation to poor quality and inefficient production.

Messes are a gold mine of opportunity for improvement. A

flow chart will help you clean up the problems and poor practices that have, over time, caused things to run off course.

Evaluate the Process

With your flow chart in hand you are now ready to evaluate the process. Do this in three steps.

1. Establish a set of expectations. What results do you expect from your target documents? How must technology perform in order to facilitate the process? How should people react upon receiving your documents? Develop your expectations from the baseline information you gathered in Chapters Three and Four. Link your expectations with the objectives of your organization and the needs of your document constituency.

2. Develop process measures that indicate whether or not your document process meets your needs and expectations. For example, what are the costs associated with each step in the document flow? How much time does it take for each step in the process to be completed? What kinds of effort, people and facilities are required to get the job done? How well is information shared or collected? Do documents actually increase customer response, boost sales or collect the correct information?

3. Collect measurement data by observing your "as-is" process in action. Do your target documents fulfill their intended purposes? Evaluate how things perform over time and collect measurable and objective data. Do your observations measure up to your expectations? Does the data you collect disprove or validate your hunches about existing problems and potential solutions? What aspects of the current process can be improved? Your aim is to determine the gaps in your process that must be overcome.

By establishing a set of expectations for each of your target documents, you set the horizon for your document strategy. By developing measures at key points in your process, you create a reference against which you can gauge the distance to your destination. By collecting objective measurement data, you are in a better position to plot a strategic route that will lead you to beneficial improvement.

Establish a Set of Expectations

Establishing expectations for each target document is the first step in uncovering the potential problems in your document process. Exactly what do you expect from your documents? This is where the effort you put into your Baseline Assessment will pay off. Consider the fundamental *business needs, pressures and constraints* that your organization must satisfy and manage. Think about the specific *objectives and strategies* of your organization as well as your overall *mission and vision*. How must your target documents perform in order to facilitate your company's success? How do your documents influence the *hard numbers* that measure company performance? How can your documents bring value to your organization rather than pose a liability – a necessary evil – that your organization must live with?

Your knowledge of your document constituency will serve you well at this step. The time you spent to identify the people involved, understand how and why they care, and build a perspective from their chair will make certain that the actions you prescribe in your strategy will "address the mess" from a real-world view. How must your documents perform in order to meet the expectations of authors, readers, producers and stakeholders? What kinds of operational constraints and pressures must be overcome? What unavoidable requirements, regulatory or otherwise, must be met?

Set Your Expectations Using "Two Wings"

To set your expectations, you may need only to pick a few important aspects such as cost, timeliness or customer satisfaction. If your situation requires that you account for a wide-ranging set of requirements and a broad combination of concerns, however, it can be more difficult to establish your exact expectations. One easy, yet comprehensive, way to assemble your expectations is to return to the concept of "Two Wings" as covered in Chapter One. Consider the following categories:

Strategic Wing

Customer response
Collecting information
Increasing sales
Brand awareness
Perceived quality and confidence
Customer satisfaction and loyalty
Leverage existing information

Tactical Wing

Cost per document
Timeliness and turnaround
Document quality
Reducing labor and effort
Reduction of errors
Reduced operating expense
Maximize investments in infrastructure

This listing, while not comprehensive, demonstrates some of the strategic and tactical aspects of your strategy. Use the information you gathered in your prior assessments to determine which strategic and tactical categories you will use. What categories should appear on your list? Add or delete items that have meaning for your particular situation. Whatever expectations you set must relate directly to the fundamental business needs, pressures and constraints of your organization. The results you seek should correspond to the requirements of your document constituency.

Do not surrender to the temptation to begin your improvement efforts before you clearly establish what you expect as a result. Defining a set of document expectations will help you avoid being pushed by management or others (or even by yourself) to come up with a quick fix rather than designing a strategy that will have lasting and meaningful benefit. Your document expectations provide a direction for your strategy, and make it possible to track the effectiveness of your actions.

Develop Process Measures

Peter Drucker, the respected management consultant, once said: "If you can't measure it, you can't manage it." You have attained a broad perspective with your earlier assessments, now take a deeper look. Process measures provide a way to observe the performance of your document process, uncover the problems that exist and monitor the results of your improvement efforts. Using your flow chart as a guide, place measures at key points in your process. Weigh these measures against the expectations you have set for your target documents to determine whether your process does, or does not, perform as you desire.

Process measures are important because they allow you to make decisions based on facts, not opinions. Your instincts and hunches may, or may not, lead you in the correct direction. A better way is to measure the performance of your target documents against the results you need. And once you implement a change, you will be better able to determine if your improvement was successful. How many times have you been involved in a project that was deemed a success, yet no one could explain exactly how things had been improved? Process measures enable you to clearly and accurately demonstrate the result of your efforts.

Types of Process Measures

Three basic types of measures can be used to gauge the effectiveness of your document process: [4]

Input measures detail the accuracy and quality of the input to your document process. Consider the saying *garbage in, garbage out*. If the original data or information that must be contained in your document is flawed, the results of your process are certain to be flawed. Input measures might include things like proofing errors, inaccurate request forms, bad data files or late batch runs.

In-process measures demonstrate how well the process is performing at certain key points within the process. Your document flow chart will help you devise measures that indicate how the various steps and functions contribute towards satisfying your expectations and the needs and objectives of your organization. In-process measures are primarily efficiency-oriented and designed to monitor operational performance. These indicators may include items such as yields, cycle times and productivity per person.

Result measures show the outcome of your process. They demonstrate document performance in concrete and observable terms. Result measures can be both quality-related and effectiveness-related, and may include things like defect rates, customer satisfaction results and sales conversion, or focus on aspects like the average time needed to prepare a document or the average number of customer complaints.

Good Data Encourages Good Decisions

Many companies collect the wrong data, if they collect any data at all. Good document performance measures satisfy the following criteria:

- **Linked to the objectives of your organization and the needs of your document constituency.** Your process measures must be closely aligned with the fundamental objectives and requirements of your organization that you established during your Baseline Assessment. Also consider the needs of your document constituency to determine the specific results you seek.

- **Measurable, countable and observable.** Develop measures that can be tracked, counted and that are not hidden from view. If it takes an extraordinary amount of effort to observe and collect measurement data, the information is likely to be of limited value and importance.

- **Easy to understand and interpret.** Process measures that are not easy to understand are of little use. Technical terms, industry jargon and financial figures are appropriate for those who understand them, but not everyone in the organization will. Design your measures so that everyone involved will have a common language with which to discuss the potential actions and benefits of your document strategy.

Case Example: XYZ Laboratories

XYZ Laboratories selects the following process measures and continues the evaluation of their monthly customer billing statements. They group their expectations into strategic and tactical categories. Customer response time, payment accuracy and leveraging existing information are selected as strategic aspects to measure. Tactical measures are cost per document, timeliness of delivery and document quality errors. They recognize customer satisfaction and maximization of equipment as important factors, but conclude that the influence of these factors does not relate exclusively to their monthly customer billing statements. In order to concentrate on the most important aspects of this target document, XYZ defines the following expectations:

Expectations

Strategic	Tactical
Customer Response	**Cost per document**
Payment received from customer within 10 days or less.	Not to exceed $0.03 (printing cost only)
Accuracy	**Timeliness**
Payment is correct no less than 99% of the time.	Document is delivered to mailroom within 24 hours upon receipt of the print job.
Leveraging existing information	**Document quality and errors**
Custom messages and promotional information issued with each bill.	Documents rerun or issued in error not to exceed .01 % of total documents.

To gather meaningful and descriptive data XYZ needed to put new input, in-process and result measures into place.

Process Measures

Measures	Results Needed
Input Measures	
The percentage of statements with incorrect billing data	No more than 1%

In-Process Measures

The average cost per document.	No more than $.03
The percentage of statements delivered within 24 hours after issue.	Target 100%
The percentage of statements . issued with custom message p/month	Target 100%

Result Measures

The average number of days before customer payment is received.	Under 10 day ave.
The percentage of statements issued with no errors.	No less than 99%
The percentage of statements that are rerun or sent in error.	No more than .01%

To put these measures into place, employees and management at XYZ must view the process in new and different ways. Determining payment accuracy means measuring the accuracy of the data supplied by the accounts payable department – a group traditionally regarded as being outside of the document process. Timeliness of customer payment requires XYZ track the time between when a specific bill is issued and when is it paid – not something previously done. Evaluating their ability to leverage corporate information requires XYZ view information processing, document design and product promotion as one overall effort, and not simply an initiative driven by the marketing department or a responsibility that falls solely on the shoulders of the IT department.

Meaningful and objective measurement data is important for making decisions and planning your strategy, but too much data can lead you off track. It is far better to have fewer meaningful measures than many ineffective measures. Some of the traps to avoid are:

- Measuring too many things.
- Spending too much time measuring.
- Measuring the wrong things.

The value of the data you gather must ultimately be weighed against the cost and effort required to collect it. W. Edwards Deming, the acknowledged guru of Total Quality

Management, warned against the dangers of overemphasizing measurement. He observed that oftentimes more effort is spent digging for data than is actually devoted to improving the process.

Many organizations focus primarily on negative measurement. Customer complaints, error rates or the cost of production reruns are certainly important measures, but it can be helpful also to include a few indicators that demonstrate positive aspects of your process as well. For instance, calculate the percentage of documents delivered on time rather than concentrating only on the number of documents that are late. Tally the dollars you save each month or the percentage you run under budget. Compute the number of customers that are happy as opposed to the number who complain. Putting a positive spin on what you do well, in addition to acknowledging the areas that need improvement, will help build credibility, support and momentum for your document strategy.

The key to developing process measures is to translate your expectations into meaningful indicators. "You can get hung up on measures that are not useful," says P.C. McGrew. "We recently worked on a European study where machine downtime, document preparation time, file transfer time and scheduling errors were all key in their process. The company's document strategy was failing because folks didn't see these factors as the root of their problems. They were focused entirely on page counts and total piece counts, and those measures did not reveal the true causes of their problem. Once we measured and observed these factors, the right solutions were clearly apparent."

Process measures are more easily found in the tactical aspects of your process. Page counts, maintenance fees and equipment capacity are concrete and easily measured. Ironically, the ease with which you can collect this data can lure you into complacency. The more important question is not how these aspects can be measured, but whether or not you have accurately defined your expectations to begin with. The strategic aspects of a document strategy are more difficult to measure and as a result are often avoided or overlooked. Measuring these more elusive aspects is an inexact undertaking so you must be creative in your approach and remain determined to find meaningful data. The real difficulty in measuring the performance of your process is not that there are too few measures that can be applied, but rather the lack of planning that is needed to measure your process in the first place.

Herein lies one very important benefit of your document strategy: The focus and forethought to observe and evaluate key behaviors of your overall document process.

Collect Process Measurement Data

Although more than half of the work force in the United States is engaged in the generation, processing, or dissemination of data, many companies do a poor job of systemically collecting appropriate data and analyzing it properly. [5] You can overcome this problem by using three tactics:

- **Use your flow chart to provide an overall picture of your process.** Bring areas for improvement into focus by placing process measures at key points in the document flow in order to spotlight hidden problems and gaps in the performance of the process.

- **Use strategic and tactical perspectives to set your expectations and develop your process**

Reality Bytes

Collecting measurement data is like collecting *reality bytes* about your process. Einstein once said that a good theory is one based on a minimum number of postulates. A document strategy must be designed in the same way – using a minimum number of assumptions without fact. Reality bytes are anti-postulates that describe reality as closely as can be. Your measurement data should describe how the process *really* works; not how it should work...or how people think it works.

Case Study: XYZ Laboratories

 XYZ collects the following "reality bytes" – measurement results that indicate how the current document process performs.

Process Measurement Data

Process measure:	The percentage of statements with incorrect billing data.
Result needed:	No more than 1%
Result observed:	Average of 5%
Process measure:	The average cost per document.
Result needed:	No more than $.03.
Result observed:	Average of $.035
Process measure:	The percentage of statements delivered within 24 hours after issue
Result needed:	Target 100%
Result observed:	Average 98%
Process measure:	The percentage of statements issued with custom message p/month.
Result needed:	Target 100%
Result observed:	Average 78%
Process measure:	The average number of days before customer payment is received.
Result needed:	Under 10 days.
Result observed:	Average of 7 days.
Process measure:	The percentage of statements issued with no print quality errors.
Result needed:	No less than 99%
Result observed:	Average 99.5%

XYZ collected measurement data over a six-month period and where ever possible used 12 months of historical data. Their measurement data uncovered areas for improvement as well as areas that performed well. Several "spikes and dips" in workload also became apparent. This perspective helped XYZ avoid making inaccurate assumptions about the overall process.

XYZ also discovered that many useful measures were already in place. The data was rarely shared outside of the individual departments, however. Simply sharing information cross-functionally enabled XYZ to bring light to aspects of their process they had not previously considered.

measures. This will not only ensure that you collect meaningful data but also that you are prepared to analyze it properly. The expectations you set for your target documents, as well as the measures you use to gauge their performance, must correlate and reflect a balance of the two essential wings of your strategy.

- **Gather data over time.** It is important to collect a broad enough sample to have meaningful averages (a few months may not be enough). Analyzing measures over time will also help to you understand and account for seasonal fluctuations and other conditions that could be misleading otherwise.

Define Problems and Determine Causes

Consider the axiom: *A problem well defined is a problem half solved.* How does the data you have collected measure up to the expectations you have set? Does your document process perform in ways, both strategically and tactically, that satisfy the needs of your organization? If the answer is no, then you must define the problems in your process, determine why each problem exists and isolate their underlying cause(s). Do this by developing a defining statement for each problem, and then use a Cause-Effect Diagram to determine why those problems plague your process.

Develop a Problem Statement

Many improvement efforts are led off track because the problems that need solving are not clearly defined. A problem statement spells out how each problem affects your process in specific terms and allows you to focus all of your energy on solving the problem rather than wasting time trying to hit a moving target. Some of the pitfalls of problems solving are: [6]

- Working on problems that are too general, too large or not well defined.
- Jumping to a solution before really understanding the problem.

- Tackling problems that are beyond your control or influence.

- Applying "pet" solutions rather than seeking a creative solution.

- Allowing your vendor to "solve" your problem for you.

- Failing to develop good reasons for choosing a solution.

You can avoid these pitfalls by developing a problem statement that objectively illustrates how the problem affects your organization and briefly summarizes where you want to be after the problem is resolved. With this approach, you define your particular problem in a way that it can be solved. The following is an example of a problem statement:

> "The average time it takes to process customer orders has increased from four days to seven days in the last 12 months. Our desired state, six months from now, is to fulfill orders within three and not increase thereafter."

A good problem statement:

- Has a desired state or goal.

- Contains measurements.

- Is "short and sweet" – no more than 40 words.

- Has no implied cause.

- Has no implied solution.

- Can pass the "So What?" test.

The example statement above clearly has a desired state – to reduce the time it takes to process orders. Specific and objective measures – from seven to three days – serve as the foundation of the statement. The authors of this statement have been brief and to the point. There are only 40 words in the statement, yet it clearly spells out the current problem and the desired state for the future.

When drafting their problem statement, the authors have been careful to avoid any reference to the cause of their problem and have not implied any kind of solution. How can anyone know the solution to a problem before they have come to terms with the problem itself and clearly understand the cause? If you assume you know the cause of your problem before you properly analyze it, you may proceed in the wrong direction. The implied cause may not be the real cause or the only cause of your problem. Here is an example of a problem statement with an implied cause:

> "Personnel turnover in the order processing department has increased the time it takes to process orders."

And here is an example of an implied solution:

> "Order fulfillment needs to be automated to accommodate for the lack of training and experience."

These may indeed be reasonable assumptions; however, the danger of beginning a problem-solving effort with an implied cause or an implied solution is that you may not find the true cause or explore all of the possible solutions. (This is especially dangerous with technology. Products that are marketed as "total solutions" may not address the real cause of your problems.)

Finally, the statement above passes the "So What?" test. Before putting time and effort into resolving a problem, ask yourself: So what? Is the problem worth solving? And if so, why? What is the impact of doing nothing? If a problem passes the "So What?" test, it is likely worth the time and effort to solve it. If you do not ask yourself the "So What?" question someone else, perhaps your boss, will. Example:

> "Order processing is taking longer...so what?" Answer: "Because our competitors will draw more customers away and we will lose money."

With answers like these, you can be assured that your problem not only exists, but it is serious and worth solving.

When developing your problem statement, ask questions like:

- **Is the problem stated objectively?** Your problem statement must not be phrased in such a way that it slants the situation in favor of one solution or another. Your statement should not leave room for interpretation. It should be a simple statement of fact.

- **Is the problem limited in scope?** Your statement must define your problem so that it is small enough for you to realistically tackle and solve.

- **Does everyone involved have a common understanding of the problem?** Your problem statement must be written so that everyone can understand it.

"The most important thing is to step back and identify the problems you are trying to solve," says Mark Wahl, who is the executive sponsor for the State of Wisconsin's award-winning document strategy. He puts problem-solving in this perspective: "You must clearly describe what your state is today, as well as what your desired state is, and then identify the gap between those two. Be very ruthless in identifying the factors that are causing the problem and separate out your assumptions. From there, analyze what actions are needed to solve the problem. It really comes down to a strategic approach to problem-solving that you can use and repeat. If you follow these steps, you have a good chance of coming up with the right solutions to the problems you find." [7]

Construct a Cause-Effect Diagram

Once you have clearly defined your problem you must determine why it exists. It is important to avoid making assumptions about the cause of your problem without spending the time and effort to dig deeper. This will limit you to studying symptoms rather than uncovering the real root cause of the problem.

The problems that occur in your process happen for a variety of reasons. These may involve things like materials, machines, methods and manpower. Other reasons may involve surroundings, suppliers, systems and skills, depending on your situation. Your aim is to isolate the root cause of the problems you identify from these many possibilities. A Cause-Effect Diagram is an important tool in this task because it assists in the generation of ideas and serves as a basis for finding the right solution. Once you identify the root cause of your problems you can direct your document strategy accordingly.

The Cause-Effect Diagram was first introduced in Japan by Kaoru Ishikawa, best known as a pioneer of the Quality Circle movement in the early 1960s. The diagram quickly became a popular tool and was widely endorsed by W. Edwards Deming and others in the field of Total Quality Management. It is a simple, graphical method for sorting out a variety of potential problem causes. The Cause-Effect Diagram is also called the Ishikawa diagram after its creator, or the fishbone diagram due to its shape.

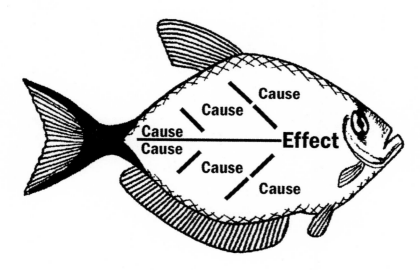

Cause-Effect, or Fishbone Diagram

A Cause-Effect Diagram will help you isolate the root cause(s) of your problem more easily.[8] The box at the right end of the diagram (the fish's head) lists the effect of your problem. This effect is, in essence, the gap you must traverse between the performance of your document process and the needs of your organization. Categories of potential causes lead off the backbone of the fish. Construct your Cause-Effect Diagram by following these three steps:

1. Identify all potential causes of the problem.

2. Determine the most likely causes.

3. Identify the root cause(s).

A brainstorming type of atmosphere may help you identify the potential causes of your problem more easily. Include the members of your document constituency who are directly involved in your document process. Share your ideas. Gather their thoughts and add them to your list. Your list of potential causes will expand as you go, then shrink as you narrow down the list to a smaller group of most likely causes. Once you have identified the most likely causes, discuss and consider each of them in detail. Eliminate the causes that don't make sense and then consolidate what is left into a short list of likely causes.

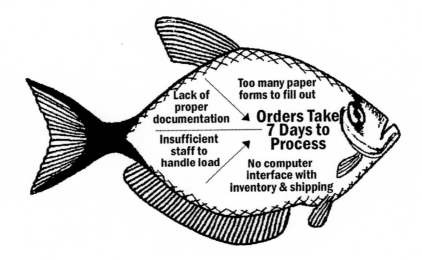

Consider the earlier problem with processing customer orders. Below is an example of a Cause-Effect Diagram with a few potential causes.

This example only lists four, but it is not unusual to have many more likely causes for your problem. Make your "fish" as big and long as it needs to be in order to contain all of the likely causes you identify. You can trim your list by repeatedly asking: *Why?* For instance, suppose one potential cause for the increase in processing time is a lack of proper documentation.

Ask: *Why is documentation important in the process?*

The answer: *Because without the proper documentation the staff will take longer to do their job.*

Follow up this response with: *Why does documentation affect the time it takes to do the job?*

The answer: *Because staff members must stop and ask for help from their co-workers and supervisors.*

Again, ask: *Why would better documentation reduce the need for assistance?*

The answer: *Because staff members could look up the procedures for themselves.*

Ask: *Why would referring to documentation speed the process?*

In this way you can zero in on the actual origin of your problem. If you do not ask these questions now, you might spend your valuable time and energy working on a solution that does not address the real root cause of your problem. It certainly seems that documentation is an issue, but could it be possible that a lack of training or experience, not necessarily a lack of proper documentation, is at the root of the problem? Could it be that the best way to increase the productivity of this group is to enable it to perform without documentation or assistance? Could it be that the origin of the problem stems from staff turnover, inadequate training, and the fact that the process needs a lot of human intervention? You will find it is not difficult to ask and answer the "Why?" question five or six times before the real root cause of your problem becomes apparent.

Questions to consider while constructing your Cause-Effect Diagram:

- Have you explored all the potential causes?

- Did you get input from the people closest to your problem?

- Are the most likely causes supported by your data?

- Did you ask "Why?" until you got to the real source of your problem?

- Does your problem statement still hold as the best statement to describe your problem?

Identify Solutions

 There are few things as useless as the right answer to the wrong question. The key to finding the best solutions for the problems you uncover is to ask the right questions. This means considering as many potential solutions to your problem as you can possibly generate and asking questions like: What are the costs associated with each solution? What are the barriers to implementation? How much time is required for implementation? What facilities, people and equipment are needed? What will be the effect on workers, managers and the company? What results are expected?

Identifying viable solutions and alternatives requires a maximum level of *informed creativity*. At this point you should be well informed and ready with a list of creative ideas to consider. When faced with a difficult problem, however, many people naturally dwell on all the constraints, rules and pitfalls that might narrow down the possible options for solving their problems. People's experience, their expectations about what will be acceptable to management, and their memories of what has worked before often restrict creativity when it comes down to the nitty-gritty of problem-solving. But often the most creative and unexpected approach brings the best results. Informed creativity means combining the information you have collected with all the possible ideas on the table, even if those ideas may seem farfetched at first.

Below is a three-step process that will aid in selecting the best possible solutions to solve your problems. In the first step, your aim is to collect a large quantity of solution ideas. Work to compile a wide-ranging list of creative ideas. In the second step, you must narrow down your list by selecting the best four to six possible solutions. In step three, you must select a final solution and one or two alternatives.

1. Generate a list of possible solutions.
2. Determine the best solutions.
3. Select a final solution (and alternatives).

Generating an all-embracing list of possible solutions will offer you a big advantage over the usual approach, which is to simply come up with two or three alternatives from which to choose. If you limit yourself to only a few alternatives you are much more likely to overlook the best solution. The two or three ideas that come quickly to mind may not actually be the best choices. A better way is to start with a much longer list of possibilities. That way, you improve your chances of exploring more innovative and unusual solutions that would not be considered otherwise.

Generate a List of Possible Solutions

Brainstorming with other people is a good way of generating a comprehensive list of creative ideas from a broad perspective. Brainstorming is a common practice, so this book does not delve into the method in detail. Nevertheless, it is important to point out that one of the difficulties with brainstorming is the natural instinct to prejudge ideas before thoroughly evaluating them. As a result, most people have a natural fear of proposing a "silly" idea or looking foolish. Ironically, silly ideas can actually form the basis for a creative and useful solution. You must strive to defer judgment and guide others in this perspective. One of the key tenets of brainstorming is that no criticism is permitted, no matter how wild and crazy suggestions seem. Encourage people to generate a large number of ideas through the combination and enhancement of existing ideas. Encourage people to key off of ideas from someone else.

One example of a successful idea that at first seemed farfetched was experienced at Kodak, where an employee approached management with the idea of making a camera so cheap and lightweight that people would throw it away after one use. The FunSaver is one of Kodak's most popular products. The idea sounded crazy at first, but the results speak for itself.

When generating a list of possible solutions, don't

stop too quickly. The first few ideas, or the most obvious ones, are not always the best. Ask yourself:

- Did you avoid passing judgment or making comments on the possible solutions as they were raised?

- Did you think outside your own experience and expertise?

- Do you fully understand each possible solution?

- Did you go for quantity – at least 20 possible solutions?

Determine the Best Solutions

Now a decision has to be made between the many solutions you have gathered. Which solutions should be included on your "short list?" Out of all the ideas you have to consider, it is likely that they are not all equally capable of producing the results you want or equally plausible to put into place. Keep in mind your goals for improvement, the expectations you have set and the key results you need. Also keep in mind what resources you have available. If you do not have the funds available for additional staff, hiring people might not be the way to go. Likewise, if you are limited on time, implementing a solution that requires many hours to put into place may not be the best option.

The following steps will help you reduce your list to a few of the best options, given your objectives and available resources:

1. Develop criteria for your selections and assign weights to each.

2. Apply the criteria.

3. Choose the best four to six solutions.

To determine the criteria to use for selecting the solutions for your short list, make sure that you define each deciding factor clearly. If you are working with a team, be sure everyone involved has the same definitions in mind. For example, you must decide whether cost is the most important criterion, or whether ease of implementation should head the list, and so on. Your criteria must also be rated in terms of importance.

Assign a weighting percentage to each criterion so that they total 100 percent. For example:

Criteria	Defined as...	Weight
Ease of implementation	How easy will it be to implement this solution?	20%
Likelihood of success	How likely is it that the solution itself can be successfully implemented?	20%
Effectiveness of Solution	How effective will the solution be in addressing the causes of the problem?	50%
Cost	How much will the solution cost compared to available funding?	10%
Total weighting		100%

Rate each possible solution against your criteria. Do this by giving each one a score on a scale of one to 10. After you have assigned a score to each factor, multiply the score by the weighting, and add up the scores for each solution.

Weighting the criteria helps you choose the best solutions to use for your final decision process. This is a very effective tool because it compares all your potential solutions objectively and guarantees equal consideration for alternative solutions. It also helps make certain someone's favorite solution does not override others. With this kind of well-thought rationale for your decisions, you should have less trouble convincing management that your recommendations are the right course for your document strategy. The questions to ask are:

- Which criteria do you need to consider?
- Are these criteria equally important?
- Does everyone involved have the same understanding of what each one means?
- Do the total weighted scores for each solution seem logical when you compare them with each other?
- Did you choose the solutions with the highest score? If not, why?

- Will you be able to persuade others that this is the right choice? If not, it's probably not the right choice.

Select a Final Solution

Now that you have a list of potential solutions, you must trim down your choices, preferably to the best four to six solutions. Do this by using a Paired-Choice Matrix similar to the one below. [9] A Paired-Choice Matrix gives you a method to choose the best solution from a number of alternatives and is an objective way to make sure each potential solution gets fair and equal consideration. One way to think of this process is like the NFL playoffs. A series of games are played between teams to determine an ultimate champion, matching one pair of teams at a time.

List your solutions on the top, as well as the left side of your matrix. In this example, six solutions have been selected (represented as A through F). Begin with the first row (Solution A) and proceed horizontally across the chart, comparing solution A to every solution along the top, one pair at a time. "X's" mark where no choice can be made (e.g., between solution A and solution A). Indicate your preferred solution by placing the corresponding letter in the corresponding column. Repeat this process until each possible pair is evaluated.

	A	B	C	D	E	F	Total
A	x	B	C	D	A	F	1
B	x	x	B	D	B	B	3
C	x	x	x	C	C	F	2
D	x	x	x	x	D	F	1
E	x	x	x	x	x	E	1
F	x	x	x	x	x	x	0
Total	–	1	1	2	0	3	x

Paired-Choice Matrix

In this example, you would start with solution A and follow the top of the matrix. Choose between A and B. (In this case solution B was selected.) Continue across the row, making a choice between A and C, A and D, and so on. Repeat the process for each row until you have compared each possible pair – compare B and A, B and C, B and D, and so on. For each row, tally the number of times that solution prevailed. Record those numbers on the right side of your matrix. Tally the scores for each column as well, and record those numbers at the bottom of the matrix. Add the numbers in the right of your matrix with the numbers at the bottom. Whichever solution has the greatest number should be your "best" solution.

In this case, the results are as follows:

```
Solution A -      1 + 0 = 1
Solution B -      3 + 1 = 4
Solution C -      2 + 1 = 3
Solution D -      1 + 2 = 3
Solution E -      1 + 0 = 1
Solution F -      0 + 3 = 3
```

With a total of four, solution B prevails. Solutions C, D and F are viable alternatives.

What happens if you have a tie? If there are three or more options with the same score repeat the process with a smaller matrix that includes only the options that have tied. If you have only two options in a tie, look for other factors that you have not previously considered. Step outside of your main focus to see if your potential solutions provide additional benefits elsewhere. Ask questions such as:

- Did you hold back from evaluating all proposed solutions?

- Did you make a point of thinking outside of your own expertise and experience?

- Did you involve others in the process – especially those who have an interest in getting the problem solved?

- Did you narrow the list to the best four to six possible solutions?

- Do you fully understand each of them?

- Do any of them need to be combined?

- What is the likelihood that your solution will be successful?

The problems you identify and the solutions you select define the course of your document strategy. Use the tools presented in this chapter to strengthen your understanding of the processes that produce your target documents, and then determine the problems that plague the process. With your problems defined, you can then determine the best solutions and plan the best route for your strategy.

Questions to Consider:

- What is the "flow" of the current process that creates your target documents?

- How must your target documents perform? What do you expect and need?

- What are the problems that prevent your document process from performing as you desire?

- Have you clearly defined those problems?

- For each problem, what is the root cause and the resulting effect?

- What viable solutions exist that will solve these problems? Which solutions are the best?

Selling Your Strategy and Managing Change

You have gone through the analysis, assessment and evaluation needed to map your plan, now you face perhaps the most difficult task of all: Selling your strategy. Support for your strategy is absolutely essential, but obtaining the sponsorship you need is not easy. Selling your strategy will require a sound business case coupled with the ability to persuasively speak in a language that will resonate with prospective supporters of your plan.

Obtaining the endorsement of executive decision-makers is only part of the challenge, however. You must also elicit the cooperation of your co-workers to make your strategy work. Regardless of sponsorship from management, if people on the front line resist change and find ways to interfere, your strategy will not take sail. Managing and implementing change will require that you anticipate the inevitable reactions people have during times of change, and that you navigate the cultural tides within your organization.

Selling Your Strategy

Even the best plan will fail without the support and resources you need to make your strategy a reality. The number one cause of death for a document strategy is a lack of sponsorship and support. That's the bad news. The good news is that you should already have the data, information and perspective you need to make a convincing case. The key is to present your case so that it will inspire and convince your prospective sponsors. "Obtaining sponsorship requires that the picture be painted in meaningful ways," says Keith Nickoloff, CEO of planetprint.com. "The picture you paint must show the benefit to the whole of the organization, especially to the extent that the results are measurable, improvement is demonstrated and cost effectiveness is enhanced. And if the brush strokes of your document strategy are in alignment with corporate direction, it will be awfully difficult to ignore." [1] When it comes to selling your strategy, the essential questions are: How do you craft a compelling portrait of your plan? What arguments will hit home with your prospective sponsors? How do you present a proposal that will win the support and resources you need?

Just as Columbus had to enlist the patronage of Ferdinand & Isabella before he could sail to the New World, you must also enlist the sponsorship of decision-makers before you embark on your journey.

Construct a Formal Proposal

You must have a persuasive proposal to sell your strategy effectively. Unless the solutions and actions you have outlined in your strategy are free of cost, you must provide clear justification for the expenditures associated with your plan. Most organizations offer limited funding for special projects and are very tightfisted with investment capital. Available funding goes quickly, so budgeting is often a competition for your fair share of the pie – project by project and purchase by purchase. To receive the funding you need, your proposal must be in a format that financial officers and executives will fully appreciate. You must communicate in terms of "dollars and sense." Decision-makers will want answers to questions like: How much will it cost? How much will we save? How long until we see a profit?

Payback

Payback is the most easily understood method for calculating return on investment and, consequently, it provides a standard criterion for determining whether to fund a project. Basically, it is the amount of time needed to recover the cost of your project. Your organization may require a specific payback time – typically between one and three years.

The example above is fairly simple, and savvy managers will be quick to point out that additional expense such as hardware

---

Case Example: XYZ Laboratories

 Suppose one component of the document strategy at XYZ is to upgrade equipment in their document production center. A new production printer is much faster than their current machine, but they must justify its purchase in order to get funding approved. Their research has established the following data:

- The current printer prints at 100 pages per minute (.00016 hours per page).

- The print speed of the new printer is 250 per minute. (.00006 hours per page)

- Current print volume is 18 million pages per year.

- The printer operator makes $10.65 per hour including benefits.

XYZ uses this data as a basis to calculate the potential annual savings and prepare a payback analysis to justify the purchase of a new printer.

Their first step is to convert printer speed from pages-per-minute to *hours-per-page*. Pages-per-minute is a common measure of printer speed, but it is necessary to reverse the data and use hours-per-page to calculate payback. This is calculated as follows:

Current printer

$$\begin{array}{r} 100 \text{ pages/minute} \\ x \quad\quad 60 \text{ minutes} \\ \hline 6{,}000 \text{ pages/hour} \end{array}$$

$$\begin{array}{r} 1 \text{ hour} \\ \div \quad 6{,}000 \text{ pages} \\ \hline .00016 \text{ hours/page} \end{array}$$

Proposed printer

$$\begin{array}{r} 250 \text{ pages/minute} \\ x \quad\quad 60 \text{ minutes} \\ \hline 15{,}000 \text{ pages/hour} \end{array}$$

$$\begin{array}{r} 1 \text{ hour} \\ \div \quad 15{,}000 \text{ pages} \\ \hline .00006 \text{ hours/page} \end{array}$$

The result of these calculations is actually a *fraction* of an hour per page. (.00016 hours for the old printer, .00006 hours for the new printer.) XYZ now uses the following equation to calculate the cost of using their old printer (current annual cost) as well as the cost of using the new printer (proposed annual cost):

Hours Per Page x Total Pages Per Year x Labor Per Hour = Cost

Current Printer Annual Cost

```
          .00016 hrs/page
x 18,000,000       pgs/year
x        10.65     per hr
     $30,672
```

Proposed Printer Annual Cost

```
          .00006 hrs/page
x 18,000,000       pgs/year
x        10.65     per hr
     $11,502
```

To calculate the annual savings that will be realized by using the new printer, XYZ subtracts the proposed annual cost from the current annual cost as follows:

Current Cost	$30,672
Proposed Cost	- 11,502
Annual Savings	$19,170

The amount saved each year is $19,170. By trading in their existing printer, XYZ is able to negotiate a purchase price for the new printer of $50,000. To determine the time it will take to pay back their investment they divide the cost of the printer by the annual savings.

$$\$50{,}000 \div 19{,}170 = 2.6$$

The time it will take to pay back the $50,000 investment is **2.6 years.**

maintenance and supplies are not included in the analysis. (These expenses could remain the same for the new printer, however.) Regardless, the method for calculating payback is relatively straightforward: Divide your investment expense by your annual savings.

The following are some additional components that you must also consider when calculating the expenses associated with your proposal:

Component	Considerations
Equipment/Capital	Types of equipment needed
	Duration required (days, months)
	Leased vs. Purchased
	Quantity needed
	Impact to overall capacity
Materials/Inventory	Raw materials needed
	Packaging
	Extra parts and supplies
	Logistics and shipping
Testing	Time needed to test
	Staff support (people, hours)
	Facilities needed
	Use of internal vs. external support
	Cost to run tests

Net Present Value and Internal Rate of Return

For more extensive projects your executive management may require a Net Present Value (NPV) and/or Internal Rate of Return (IRR) analysis. NPV and IRR are two measures that describe the return on investment of your proposal in terms that financial officers and decision-makers understand. In many organizations, if you do not include this type of financial analysis, or if it is deemed incomplete, your proposal will be rejected or returned for additional work. One senior executive puts it this way: "We evaluate all sizable funding proposals

based on two things, return on investment and our priorities."
In many cases, NPV and IRR are the only quantifiable ways to
evaluate the financial impact of your project. The methods are
fairly complicated, so it is best to work with your company's
financial experts. The following attempts to present these
concepts in an understandable form.

Net Present Value (NPV)

NPV can be defined as the future benefits and costs of your
proposal converted into equivalent values today. This is done
by assigning a dollar value to the benefits and costs associated
with your plan, discounting those benefits and costs using an
appropriate discount rate, and subtracting the sum total of
discounted costs from the sum total of discounted benefits.

That explanation sounds complicated for a very good reason:
It is. Think of NPV as simply today's dollar value of all the
future costs and benefits of your project...taking into account
your "opportunity cost." Cost of capital, or opportunity cost,
sounds complex, but it is simply a measure (in percentage) of
what your company forgoes when it chooses to do something.
The concept of opportunity cost is central to corporate decision-
making. When evaluating your request, your management
must consider a variety of other opportunities. Your proposal
competes not only with other projects on the docket, but many
other courses of action available – including doing nothing.

Internal Rate of Return (IRR)

IRR is the percentage discount rate that, if applied to your
project's future cash flows (positive and negative), returns
a NPV of $0. As a rule, a positive NPV (greater than $0)
indicates that your project is of economic benefit and should
be pursued. If your project has a negative NPV, it does not
provide sufficient positive cash flow to cover the expense of the
project as well as your organization's opportunity cost. In this
event, it is unlikely that your proposal will be accepted.

In other words, if your organization uses 10% cost of capital
for project evaluation (a fairly standard percentage), proposals
with an IRR above 10% would be pursued. One way to
look at IRR is to consider that your organization's Wall Street

investments will likely gain 10% or more. If your IRR is below 10%, it would be more profitable to leave the money in the bank.

Naturally, a financial analysis is probably not the only factor your firm will use in deciding whether your proposal should be funded. Scoring committees often use a weighted scoring that ranks each project for its effectiveness in achieving certain strategic goals. Financial performance is only one – albeit a very important one – of those scoring criteria.

Data Required to Calculate NPV and IRR

In order to calculate NPV and IRR (using Microsoft Excel functions) the following information is required.

- Positive cash flows (benefits).

- Negative cash flows (costs).

- Net cash flows (the difference between the benefits and the costs).

- The timing of the cash flows (by month or quarter).

- The organization's opportunity cost of capital (percentage discount rate).

The XYZ case is a relatively simple example. However, the principle of quantifying net cash flow and applying the NPV and IRR formulas is exactly the same whether your project involves ten thousand dollars or ten million.

Put it in Writing

Any proposal worth considering must be in written form. If you make a formal request verbally, or without clearly written justification, your proposal may be viewed more as complaining and whining than as a meaningful plan. Even the best ideas will be of limited value if you do not communicate them effectively. Written proposals that are well organized and competently researched are more likely to get attention and acceptance. By presenting your case in writing, you will build management's confidence in your proposal and inspire trust in your abilities.

Case Example: XYZ Laboratories

XYZ proposes a project that will require an up front investment of $75,000 for document composition software. Staff time for programming and implementation will cost an additional $20,000 over six months. A ¼ full time employee (FTE) will be needed to maintain the project throughout its three-year life. The opportunity cost of capital (discount rate) is 10%. The benefit of the project is that the organization will be able to eliminate 2 FTE positions.

The cash flows by quarter are shown on the next page.

Using MS Excel functions, the NPV and IRR calculate as follows:

```
NPV (rate,value1,value2, ...)
```

NPV = $5,190

The present value of all future cash flows (given the XYZ's 10% cost of capital) is $5,190. Since the value is greater than $0, the project is financially beneficial to the organization.

```
IRR (values, guess) ²
```

IRR = 13.19%

The IRR of 13.19% is greater than the 10% opportunity cost of capital, so this is a beneficial project. Another way of looking at this is to say that the project will "make" 3.19% (13.19% minus 10%).

Your write-up does not have to be long and elaborate. In fact, the more concise the better. Successful proposals can be as brief as one page (see sample below) if your approach is sound. It is possible that after weeks of analysis and multiple revisions to a lengthy proposal, the request that is ultimately accepted is the one that can be summarized with a number two pencil and a yellow legal pad. In most organizations, however, only a formal written proposal will attract the serious consideration that can lead to funding and resources for your project.

The following is an outline for an effective written proposal:

Case Example Spreadsheet

	Q1	Q2	Q3	Q4	Q5	Q6	Q7	Q8	Q9	Q10	Q11	Q12	Q13	Q14
Development & Implementation														
New Hardware	(75000)													
Staff Time ($'s)	(10000)	(10000)												
Ongoing Support														
Staff Time 1/4 FTE ($'s)			(15000)	(15000)	(15000)	(15000)	(15000)	(15000)	(15000)	(15000)	(15000)	(15000)	(15000)	(15000)
Total Cash Outlays	(85000)	(10000)	(15000)	(15000)	(15000)	(15000)	(15000)	(15000)	(15000)	(15000)	(15000)	(15000)	(15000)	(15000)
Project Benefits														
2 FTE Reduction ($'s)			25000	25000	25000	25000	25000	25000	25000	25000	25000	25000	25000	25000
Net Cash Flow	(85000)	(10000)	10000	10000	10000	10000	10000	10000	10000	10000	10000	10000	10000	10000

- Executive Summary
- Recommendation
- Discussion
  - Scope
  - Objectives
  - Costs and Benefits
  - Financial Analysis
  - Alternatives
- Suggested Implementation Schedule

Begin your proposal with an *executive summary* that provides a brief background that summarizes the current situation and indicates the reason for your proposition. Follow this immediately with your *recommendation*. Never put your recommendation at the end of your report. Your proposal is not a novel with a surprise ending, so be up front about what you are asking for and why. Because the executive summary and recommendation are the essence of your proposal, you must get to your point quickly and be specific. Your proposal must be succinct, have substance and be compelling. You must accomplish this in your first few paragraphs or risk losing the interest of decision-makers.

The body of your proposal should contain discussion paragraphs that explain the *scope* of your project (what it does and does not cover) as well as your specific *objectives* (in measurable terms). Detail the *costs and benefits* associated with your proposal and include a *financial analysis*. Be sure to offer some *alternatives* to your primary recommendation. Are there other ways to address the situation other than your first choice? Explain the consequences of doing nothing. What will happen if your proposal is not adopted?

Conclude your paper with a *suggested implementation schedule*. Be sure to include specific milestones and measurements. Show that you have thought through the implementation of your plan and that it can be accomplished successfully. One word of caution: Be realistic about your projections. Don't sugarcoat your recommendation in order to get approval only to find that you can't deliver when the time comes.

Sample Proposal: XYZ Laboratories

Using the previous payback analysis for a new printer, XYZ presents the following written proposal as a request for funding:

April 15, 2001

To: David Carlson, Vice President of Operations, XYZ Laboratories

From: Lisa Ness, Manager, Document Services

Subject: New production printer for the document center

Executive Summary

We use a seven year-old production printer to print bills, statements, checks and an assortment of other critical documents. This machine prints at approximately 100 pages per minute. New printers can print at 250 pages per minute (and more). I propose that we replace our old printer with a new model. This proposal contains the results of my analysis.

Recommendation

I recommend that we spend $50,000 to purchase a new, higher speed, printer. The attached financial analysis shows that we can save an estimated $19,170 per year. The investment has a payback under 3 years (2.6). In addition, there are a number of other benefits that will be realized with the new printer.

Discussion

This new printer will enhance our ability to meet ever-tightening print turnaround expectations. I have visited other companies that have this printer and found that it performs well in similar environments. It will afford us a 150% increase in printing speed.

The impact of installing this new printer will be minimal since it is compatible with existing systems. This is intended as a one-for-one replacement for our current printer (volume 18 million per year). My aim is to shorten our turnaround time by a minimum of 50% and ultimately as much as 150%. There will be no internal support needs since the vendor will remove our old machine and install the new one (included in purchase). Our operators will not need any additional training; the new printer is essentially the same as the old one, only faster.

Please see the attached installation plan. We can install and test the new printer in one week. Disruption to our work will be minimal. The only impact we anticipate is with our weekly statement run (on Mondays), but we feel that we can cover the workload using our other printers and approximately 10 hours of overtime.

As an alternative, we could continue to use our old printer. It requires quite a bit of maintenance, however. Downtime has increased nearly 25% over the past 12 months. On several occasions recently, it has been down for extended periods of time. This is especially troublesome during the first of the month, which is our busiest time. Existing owners of the new printer indicate a dramatic reduction in maintenance and downtime and are more than satisfied with its performance.

We should realize the following benefits:

- We will decrease our turnaround time and increase our print capacity.

- Maintenance and downtime will be reduced.

- The new printer is more technologically up-to-date and will work well with new data processing systems.

- Errors will be reduced due to additional automation features.

- Employee morale will be improved.

Respectfully submitted,

Lisa Ness

Manager, Document Services

Speak the Language

To stimulate sponsorship and support, you will need more than just facts and figures. To sell your strategy, you must "speak the language" of the people you aim to convince. You must learn who your prospective sponsors are, what aspects of your strategy will be most compelling to them and how to best communicate your ideas and recommendations. Get inside their frame of reference and speak persuasively in a dialect that will resonate with their views. Be prepared to discuss the right things at the right times.

Just as knowing your document constituency is necessary while designing your strategy, knowing your sponsors is an essential part of selling your strategy. If your sponsor is a stickler for statistics and closely watches the bottom-line, sell him with hard numbers. If your sponsor is concerned with things like customer service, perceived quality or brand image, you might concentrate on how communications will be enriched, how customers will be more satisfied and how the image of the company will be enhanced. If your sponsor has a technological focus, concentrate on how your strategy will keep current with the curve of innovation and take advantage of trends in technology.

Whatever the context, you must recognize and be fluent in the various "languages" that will communicate effectively with your prospective sponsors and inspire commitment. You may need to speak different languages at different times, even with the same sponsor. And speaking the wrong language, or lingering too long in one, will quickly dispel enthusiasm for your strategy. The question is: What language will ring true with your prospective sponsors...and why?

Find the Emotion

One approach is to "find the emotion" that will connect your strategy with the person you are trying to convince. Dr. Keith Davidson of Xplor International describes this notion in terms of a skillfully scripted political campaign. "A practiced politician will focus on the issues that strike an emotional chord with constituents. For instance, when giving a speech to members of the Veterans of Foreign Wars, he'll stress the need

Consider the Mazda Miata. Legend has it that the designer was having trouble convincing Mazda executives to move forward with development of the ragtop. Market studies, schematics and specifications failed to inspire the level of support needed. One sunny day the designer took a top executive on a drive down a curvy road in a cherry red British MGB. With the top down and the wind in their hair, the designer simply said: "This is the experience we should build." The Miata, now regarded as a modern classic, is a legendary success for Mazda.

for a strong national defense. The same speech delivered on a college campus will stress peacekeeping with an all-volunteer army. This type of 'spin' is not really a matter of deception, but rather a matter of addressing the essence of what people really care about." [3]

Beware of Jargon

Industry jargon and technical terminology are effective ways to communicate when used in the correct context, but your sponsors will probably be less interested in the bits and bytes of your proposal than the benefits and risks your strategy presents. Beware of the tendency to overuse jargon. Selling your strategy will depend on your ability to speak in terms of the positive impact on your organization, not your ability to explain how each technical component works. In most circumstances, not everyone will understand (or care to understand) technical terminology, so it is best to leave jargon for focused interactions with people who thrive on the lingo. Otherwise, you run the risk of both boring and confusing the people you are trying convince.

Another danger presented by jargon arises when you are not familiar with the terms. If you do not have the benefit of a high-tech background it can be hard to keep up with the vernacular of technology, especially when technology evolves at such a rapid pace. This can put you at a disadvantage. Certainly, in-depth knowledge is best left for the technical experts. Nevertheless, to sell your strategy, you must have a fairly fluent understanding of the technological language involved. If you do not, you must work to expand your vocabulary – take notes, keep your ears open and do not be afraid to ask questions when you do not understand something. Even when the techno-babble seems endless, irrelevant and foreign, take advantage of the opportunity to learn the language.

Be Concise

Unless you work in the executive suite, your exposure to decision-makers is probably limited. It can be helpful to develop a brief mental summary of the most outstanding benefits of your strategy. Think of this as an "elevator pitch." Imagine you enter an elevator in the lobby of your building and bump into the CIO – the very person you've been hoping to enlist as a sponsor. You have exactly three minutes before the elevator reaches the 15th floor. This may be your best and only opportunity to pitch your ideas. If you can be convincing and compelling in this brief time – X will improve Y because of Z – those three minutes may be all you need to get the support you need.

Prepare yourself to take advantage of unplanned opportunities to enlist support. Your ability to summarize your strategy (or at least the major benefits) concisely will be helpful in meetings and other conversations as well. You may have only a few moments during a meeting to discuss your concepts. Your "elevator pitch" will be useful in the hallway, or at the local Starbuck's, as well as in the executive boardroom.

Build Co-Worker Buy-In

You also must have the buy-in of your peers and co-workers for your strategy to be successful. Everyone involved with your document process, from entry-level clerks to high-level specialists, must support your strategy (or, at the very least, not sabotage your efforts). This is especially true for people who are the target of the changes you propose. Your ability to inspire co-worker support depends on your ability to answer:

What's in it for me? For these people, the "proof is in the pudding." You must prove that your strategy will make their job easier, less chaotic and more productive. You must demonstrate how improvements will directly benefit their department. You must show them that day-to-day operations will be made better and that everyone will benefit from your plan.

Testimonials

One way to build buy-in is to elicit *testimonials* from people who have benefited from earlier improvements. Enlisting others to validate and verify your success is a powerful way to create momentum and support for your strategy. Testimonials can help you overcome resistance to change and convert skeptics to your cause. "Behavior is the hardest thing to change. You are not going to change somebody if they don't want to change," says Tom Martino from Warner-Lambert. "The way we do it is to find a champion to provide a testimonial. So rather than try to sell an overall concept or theory, we leverage the testimony and enthusiasm of those people whose job has been made better. If we can get them to say 'this is great, I don't know why we didn't do it years ago,' then we inspire grass roots support for our strategy." [4]

The testimony of satisfied co-workers and colleagues will enhance your reputation and credibility. The more testimonials you collect, the more credibility you gain. Your aim is for cynics to observe improvement in other areas of the company and decide that they want to get in on the benefits being realized by other people. To raise awareness within your company you will need to do a certain amount of self-promotion. Be assertive and creative in your effort to get the word out about your successes. "We advertise testimonials and successes in a variety of ways," says Martino. "Since we are the division of the company that knows how to communicate, it's not difficult to find ways to get the word out. We use a combination of printed materials, our electronic bulletin board and our Intranet."

Use testimonials to continually expand your circle of supporters and sponsors – at both higher and grass roots levels. Look for people who are willing to testify how their job or department has been improved and how the company is more profitably served by your strategic efforts.

Piggyback on Important Initiatives

 Another way to sell your strategy is to *piggyback* on other important initiatives underway in your company. From your Baseline Assessment, you should have a good understanding of the major projects and programs being considered. To piggyback, link an aspect of your strategy with an initiative that has a high degree of importance to your company or to a particular department. Show how you can help meet the objectives of the project. Look for new ways of doing things that will overcome the challenges and barriers that prevent implementation of the project. Craft a document solution that makes a difference and contributes to a specific vision or objective. The more you are able to piggyback on the strategic agenda of other areas in your organization the more likely it is that you will find willing supporters and sponsors. The questions are:

- What aspects of your strategy feed into important corporate initiatives?

- What new ideas for your strategy are needed to serve the initiatives that are planned?

- What features serve the objectives of other departments and sponsors?

- Which of your recommendations line up with important items on their agenda?

You may find that some aspect of your strategy suddenly becomes more valuable than you first thought. For instance, a particular solution or project may not have been your first choice to pursue, but if you find that it aligns closely with an important initiative or fits within the agenda of another department you are more likely to get a green light for your ideas. It is also possible that recommendations you made months or even years earlier will take on a new dimension of importance. The corporate landscape is replete with levelheaded recommendations that collect dust in an in-basket until they abruptly become part of someone else's agenda.

Until another driving need comes along, even the best ideas can go unnoticed. Another possibility is that an important initiative will add new requirements that you did not consider. New ideas and solutions may be needed to serve a particular need. Piggybacking is another way of making certain your strategy is aligned with the most important initiatives and objectives of your company.

Managing Change

The Roles in a Successful Change Initiative

Once you have the approval to move forward with your strategy, there are five roles that people perform that are critical to your success. As the person who is leading the initiative to change, you perform in the role of *change agent*. A *change sponsor* is the executive decision-maker who has sanctioned the change and approved the resources needed for your strategy. The people who actually implement new technology and execute alterations in your process are *change enablers* – the experts needed to make changes happen. The people directly impacted by the changes you propose are *change targets*. A *sustaining sponsor* carries on the revised process and assures that the improvements put into place continue to provide their intended benefit.

Characteristics of the roles of change:

Change Agent

- Responsible for the implementation of the change.
- Responsible to "educate" the sponsor in terms of what is needed to successfully implement the change.
- Acts as team leader, keeper of the research and is the expert regarding the change initiative.
- Assembles the needed resources (people, funding and equipment) in order to fulfill change objectives.

Change Sponsor

- Has authority and ability to sanction the change.
- Can commit the needed resources to the project.
- Will apply pressure to overcome barriers and reward supportive performance.
- Will "fly the flag" with other executives and board members as needed.
- Will openly demonstrate support and endorsement of the change.

Change Enabler

- The expert resource needed to implement new technology or changes in the current process.
- Possesses the knowledge and skill to make change happen.
- Acts as a consultant and team member.
- Provides technical and detailed information when needed.
- Provides ideas for improvements and enhancements to existing ideas and solutions.

Change Target

- The individual or group that must actually change.
- Will either embrace or resist change.
- Must assume accountability for the change to be successful.

Sustaining Sponsor

- Responsible for the ongoing process.
- "Takes the ball" once the change has been implemented.
- Responsible for continuous measurement and re-evaluation.

Change Agent

If you are designing a document strategy, you are a change agent. You are proposing and advocating for a change in the way things are normally done. Once you successfully obtain the approval to move forward with your plan, your primary role is to educate your sponsor. Your sponsor must clearly understand what is needed in order to make the change successful. It is your job to communicate the resources that you need, the barriers that stand in your way and the people that must be enlisted in the change initiative. At the same time, you must be responsive to the expectations of your sponsor as you move forward in the process.

Educating your sponsor can be a very difficult situation, especially if he or she outranks you and is not giving you the support and resources you need or that were promised. At times, you may need to go back to your sponsor and clarify what your sponsor must do to meet that need. You might imagine how this could develop into a touchy state of affairs. For instance, your executive board may think your strategy is a great idea and assign a sponsor, but if your sponsor either doesn't care or doesn't get it, your strategy will fail. If you do not get what you need from your sponsor, should you go up to the board to twist the arm of your sponsor? You may have to take that risk if you want your strategy to succeed. The opposite case may be true where you have a strong and supporting sponsor who must continually return to the executive board and reiterate the importance and benefit of your strategy in order to keep things moving.

Change Sponsor

A change sponsor is the person in authority who has given approval for the change. The sponsor of your strategy has the authority to provide funding and resources to your project and the power to both reward and reprimand. An effective sponsor must:[5]

- Feel dissatisfied with the way things are currently.

- Have a clear definition of what should be changed.

- Believe that change needs to occur.

- Understand the long-term impact your strategy will have on the organization.

- Understand what people are being asked to change about the way they operate.

- Understand the resources that are needed for the change to be successful.

- Display the type of public support needed to convey strong commitment to the change.

- Be willing to use influence and authority to eliminate roadblocks.

- Be willing to reward those who support the change and express displeasure with those who resist.

- Ensure that progress is tracked and monitored.

- Show consistent and sustained support for the change.

In addition, a sponsor legitimizes your role as change agent by vesting his or her authority to you by proxy. In this way, your sponsor gives you the authority to apply the necessary changes, allocate the appropriate resources and direct the work of others. In essence, your sponsor is the champion of change and passes sponsorship and authority to you. Your job is to confirm that your sponsor is well informed and committed to do what it takes for your strategy to be successful.

Change Enabler

A change enabler is the person or department with the knowledge and skill to actually make changes in the current process. In most cases, you will need experts to implement new technology and people who are experienced in and responsible for the current process in order to put your plans into practice. Change enablers are valuable team members who provide critical counsel and information. Rely on these experts to provide detailed information about technology and perspective on existing or reengineered business processes.

Change Target

A change target is the person or group who must change as a result of your strategy. Change will target specific people and workgroups whenever you implement new equipment, systems or processes. People may resist change for a variety of reasons that are explored later in this chapter, but ultimately, they must embrace the needed changes if your strategy is to be successful. How readily they accept these changes will depend on how effectively they are made to understand how the given changes will benefit them, and how successfully your sponsor legitimizes the need to change.

Sustaining Sponsor

Once a change has been put into place a sustaining sponsor is needed to assure that the new process continues to perform as it should. A sustaining sponsor takes the ball and continues to score points with the improvements that have been put into place. It is important that responsibility is passed to a sustaining sponsor since even the most innovative change will not survive and thrive if it is not sustained over time. Sustaining sponsors are responsible for the continuous improvement of the process, and measuring and monitoring the process in action. They must adjust and revise whatever changes have been made so that as conditions vary, operations and functions follow accordingly.

What are the various roles people need to play for your strategy successful? What is your role? Will these roles remain static, or will they change depending on the situation?

It is likely that you will need to function in more than one role during the process of implementing your strategy. Your role is primarily that of a change agent, but you also may have the authority and accountability to sponsor change. Or perhaps you will be the eventual target of the very changes you propose and ultimately function as a sustaining sponsor. Depending on your situation, you must be prepared to wear these many "hats" as needed, and expect that others will need to do so as well.

Sponsorship is Critical

Strong, effective sponsorship is critical to the success of any change initiative. "Finding support and sponsorship is essential, but it is the most difficult aspect of a document strategy," says Barry Lietuvnikas, systems analyst for the City of Baltimore. "It can be frustrating when you feel like you are beating people over the head about the value of documents, but very little headway gets made. While I've been able to raise awareness somewhat, I often run into roadblocks because I don't have the sponsorship I need." [6]

Some people might argue that change does not always have to be mandated from the top. It is true that beneficial change can happen from a grass roots beginning, but if your document strategy requires financial or human resources you inevitably will need the support of a sponsor who is both willing and has the authority to authorize the use of those resources. Without that level of support, your strategy will be limited only to incremental improvements when they present themselves within your area of control or influence.

"My philosophy about an enterprise document strategy is beginning to hit home, but until I get the support I need from above, I continue to get overridden on many fronts," says Lietuvnikas. "I'm able to make improvements within my area, but as for an overall strategy, we probably won't spend the time to do things right and end up doing a lot of things over again."

Contracting

One thing that will guarantee the failure of your strategy is the lack of effective *contracting*. You must make effective agreements between the various people involved in your project and monitor and revise those contracts over time. For example, a change agent and a change sponsor have an agreement that spells out who will do what and when, as does the agreement between a change agent and change enablers. A similar contract exists between sponsors, sustaining sponsors and the people who are the target of change. Any breakdown or miscommunication with regard to these virtual contracts can cause your strategy to fail, so contracting must be attended to with diligence and understanding.

When contracting, you must establish the expectations of each relationship as well as goals of your agreement. Be clear about what you expect and when. Your strategy is a work in progress so these commitments need to be renegotiated as conditions change. Otherwise, what may happen over time is that your expectations could be very different from your sponsor's expectations or the expectations of the people who are the target of change. Your notion of how things should look might be very different from those of the people implementing changes and sustaining the new process.

If you are not effective at contracting at your level of authority, you may need to approach your sponsor and ask for his or her involvement. Either way, if people do not live up to their commitments, your efforts will not be effective.

Tips for Managing Change

Implementing change and overcoming obstacles requires anticipation, patience and perspective. Resistance to change is inevitable, so rather than fight it; expect it, acknowledge it and respect it. The challenges and techniques of managing change are much too broad to cover in this book, [7] but it is important to acknowledge some of the critical factors that must be addressed in order to successfully implement your strategy:

- **Develop a true commitment to the change.** Consider the axiom: *Those convinced against their will are of the same opinion still.*

- **Dedicate sufficient resources to manage the change.** In addition to putting effort and money into things like hardware or software, don't forget to set aside proper time and resources to deal with the reactions of people who are the target of change.

- **Monitor and adjust in response to problems.** Just as Columbus had to periodically adjust his course to accommodate for trade winds and ocean currents, you must adjust your actions in response to problems and changing business conditions.

- **Overcome old habits.** The habits associated with "we've always done it this way" are hard to break.

- **Manage change by principle, not expediency.**
  Don't expect change to happen over night. It takes
  time and a clear, unwavering direction.

- **Cultivate support through skillful, sensitive
  interactions.** Learn to speak the language that will
  connect with each individual who must support
  the change.

Incremental Change vs. Transformational Change

There are two kinds of change: Incremental and
Transformational. Does your document strategy plan for a
series of small, incremental changes over time? Or does it
involve large-scale change that will transform a major aspect
of the way you do business today? Incremental change and
transformational change are significantly different in nature
and must be managed and facilitated in different ways.
Incremental change does not require sponsorship. You may
not need to ascend to the top of the organizational chart
or establish a widely felt need. *Transformational change,*
on the other hand, requires that the leadership of your
company dramatically demonstrate commitment to the change.
The perception must be that immediate success is critical.
Incremental change can be accomplished "out of pocket,"
working on improvements as funding or resources become
available in the day-to-day operation of your business.
Transformational change requires that your company maintain
focus on a single, grand theme for change.

Here are some of the defining characteristics of incremental and
transformational change:

Incremental Change	**Transformational Change**
Does not challenge assumptions and values of existing culture.	Attempts to alter the existing culture.
Modifies and slightly improves overall operations.	Focuses on significant reengineering and improvement.
Uses existing structures, procedures and processes.	Challenges the relevance of existing structures, procedures and processes.

Minor disruption to the status quo.

Dramatically alters the status quo.

Relatively low risk.

Relatively high risk.

The Cycle of Change

One very influential factor that can potentially undermine your document strategy is the natural and emotional reactions of people when things change.[8] It is common to take great care in the selection and implementation of new technology. Interactions between hardware and software are cautiously investigated, operating systems and network connections are carefully tested, and up time on critical systems is painstakingly protected. But if people resist change, find ways to sabotage efforts, or become angry or withdrawn, it is much less likely that your strategy will have meaningful success.

Resistance to change is often a more troubling problem than even the most complicated tangle of technology. To make matters worse, rapid innovation in technology is forcing people to face change at an ever-quickening pace. This rapidity, coupled with the apparently inevitable and chronic "technical difficulties" associated with high-tech change, has given rise to a pattern of resistance that has become a norm of corporate culture. Most people automatically resist change. How can you mitigate the negative effects of people's reactions as you implement change and execute a document strategy?

Resistance to Change is Natural

Roger Von Oech said it best when he said: *"There are two basic rules of life: Change is inevitable and everybody resists change."* [9] Resistance to change is as congenital as being frightened of the dark, having a crush at age sixteen or laughing at the Three Stooges. Little can be done to avoid these reactions. They are natural, emotional and inevitable. This innate resistance to change occurs because most people like things to be comfortable and familiar. They like to feel capable and confident in their work. Imagine the impact of change on the ability of people to feel comfortable, capable and confident. Your document strategy can upset all of these factors – people must learn new systems, work in new ways and accept new responsibilities.

People facing change often go through a cycle of emotions similar to those experienced when faced with the death of a loved one.[10] Enacting change is somewhat less disturbing. Nevertheless, by understanding the "grieving" process people use to deal with change you will be better prepared to lessen some of the potentially damaging consequences.

Consider the cycle of emotions that people are likely to experience when faced with change.

The Comfort Zone

"The Comfort Zone" is where people reside emotionally before dramatic change occurs. When people are in their comfort zone, they feel in *control* of their lives and work. Generally, they are happy and *comfortable* with the way things are. They are *confident* in their abilities and feel *capable* of handling whatever situations arise. Will you disrupt employees' comfort zones by changing the methods and routines of their work? When people are asked to use new processes and perform new duties, they may feel that their control over their work is diminished. They might lose confidence when "the way we've always done it" gives way to something new and unknown.

Are these people laggards who are unwilling to join the cause of improvement and innovation? Not necessarily. Most people would rather feel a little bit stagnant, complacent and bored than face the possibility of losing their comfort zone.

To assist you in the Comfort Zone:

- Notice the situations in which you experience ease and comfort.
- Notice the situations in which you experience stagnation and a lack of growth.
- Create a development plan for the situations you want to change.

To assist others in the Comfort Zone:

- Encourage creativity and cross-functional innovation.
- Acknowledge, celebrate and reward success.
- Plan for future changes.

The No Zone

"No!" is the common reaction of people who face departure from their comfort zone. The "No Zone" is the beginning of the end of the way things always have been and is characterized by several reactions.

Shock

Like deer frozen in the headlights of an oncoming pickup truck, people often become psychologically paralyzed at the news of change in their work-lives. Their shock immediately affects their performance. Although the basic work gets done, people tend to shut down. How do you help people break their trance-like stare into the onrushing headlights of change? When people are physically in shock we cover them with a warm blanket. What people need now, in psychological terms, is also a "warm blanket." Now is not the time to reason with them about all the ways change is good. Now is the time for emotional first aid – listening and understanding "where it hurts" will help mitigate the trauma of change.

Denial

After their initial shock, people may enter a stage of denial. This defense mechanism acts as a buffer and allows people to collect themselves. It is not uncommon to hear comments like: "This won't affect our department," or "I give it six months and it'll pass." At times, denial can take form in extensive rituals. For example, a person may ardently dispute the findings of a report and claim that the data must be in error – or insist that endless meetings be held (and then not show up). Some people, like patients unhappy with their doctor's diagnosis, will shop around with other managers or sponsors until they find someone with a more reassuring second opinion.

Anger

When they can no longer deny the inevitable, people often become angry. Anger is difficult to manage because it can be channeled in so many different directions and thrust into the workplace almost at random. In contrast to denial, which is for the most part internalized to an individual, a person who is angry affects everyone around him. One way you can cope is by placing yourself in the shoes of that angry person. Where does the anger come from? A person who is respected and understood, who is given attention and a little time, will soon lower his voice and reduce his angry demands.

Resentment, Frustration and Sabotage

Some of the anger people feel may manifest as *resentment, frustration* or *sabotage*. People may resent you for upsetting their comfort zone. They may secretly envy those in charge and feel frustrated that their control has been eroded. They may become passive-aggressive and subtly sabotage efforts by doing nothing, hoarding information or providing erroneous information. People may truly disrespect those in authority based upon their experience if the actions of management have been ineffective in the past.

The "No-Zone" is an emotional phase. It is difficult and delicate for everyone involved. Resistance to change is at its peak. Those who are the target of change will not be willing to plan for the future. A dialogue must take place before you plan, but only when people are ready to face it.

It is equally important, however, that resistive people not hold you and the project hostage. If you believe your motives are sound and your solutions are viable, it is more important now than ever that you hold your course. Don't let the naysayers drag you down.

To assist you in the No Zone:

- Identify the reality of the situation.
- Acknowledge the losses you are experiencing.
- Identify your feelings about the situation.
- Reframe "danger" into "opportunity."

To assist others in the No Zone:

- Give information about the purpose for the change.
- Provide a picture of the expected outcome.
- Provide clear and specific expectations.
- Provide a historical context.
- Be there for others in small, supportive ways.
- Listen to worries and fears.

The Gap

People in "The Gap" are people in limbo. They know they can't go back, but each wonders: "How do I fit in this picture?" You must allow people to reflect and discover their own view about how they are a part of things. Foster this process by helping people understand their role in the change and how they can make it successful. Do this with education, and training, and by planning people-specific roles.

It is imperative that you establish a vision for the future while in the gap, and then enact specific tactics to achieve that vision. A clear plan is critical because people in the gap are people sitting on the fence. They are not necessarily resisting change, but they have not given their complete commitment either. Now is the best opportunity to bring fence sitters through the gap to acceptance. Without an understanding about where things are going and how everyone will get there, the opportunity to build commitment and acceptance for your document strategy will be lost.

Bargaining

Some people accept change quickly. Others figure that since denial and anger didn't work, perhaps they can succeed in entering into some sort of agreement that will postpone the inevitable. For example, if a four-year-old does not get his way, he will stomp his foot and go sulk in his room. He will not accept "No" when he wants ice cream for breakfast. Soon, he'll have second thoughts and put on extra-good behavior. "If I pick up all my toys, *then* can I have ice cream?" he'll eventually ask. Grown-up people will bargain too. They will bargain for ways to get back to their comfort zone.

Depression

People in the gap also experience depression. It is important to draw a distinction between two kinds of depression – reactive and preparatory – since each is different in nature and should be dealt with quite differently.[11]

Reactive depression happens when people are reacting to, and becoming depressed by, the things that are taking place. They are worried about how change will affect the basics like money, job and family. The "downside" of change – reassignment, retraining and reengineering – is evident, but even the "upside" has drawbacks. For instance, a golden opportunity presented to one lucky overachiever may actually result in a loss of precious family time at home. While the new job may look good on paper, this change represents a potentially disruptive force on a personal level. Any change, even positive change, results in a loss of something – tangible or intangible. Your can alleviate the effects of reactive depression by recognizing how change can strike home for an individual.

Preparatory depression, on the other hand, does not occur as a result of what is presently happening, but rather, as the emotional process of preparing for what is ahead. If you allow people to grieve for the old ways they will find acceptance of the new much easier. Preparatory depression is necessary for people to get ready for the impending change, yet the typical reaction to sad people is to try to cheer them up. "Look on the bright side" can be a useful approach when dealing with reactive depression, but when the depression is helping to prepare a person for impending change, cheery words are not meaningful. To look only at the sunny side of things means people are not allowed to contemplate how they fit in the picture of impending change.

Anxiety

By now people recognize that things are not going to be the way they were, but they don't yet know the shape of the future. They are anxiously torn, part hanging on to the old, while another is accepting the new. When people feel *anxious* about their jobs, uncertain about where to place their trust and unclear about the future, honest communication is critical. You must have the courage to describe reality as closely as possible to what you know reality to be. People need to know how change will impact their lives. If people are afraid of the dark, give them a flashlight and do your best to assure them there are no monsters hiding under the bed.

To assist you in The Gap:

- Discover what *you* want for the future.
- Get necessary information and support.
- Don't let the naysayers drag you down.

To assist others in The Gap:

- Create "rites of passage."
- Create temporary procedures.
- Create new ways for people to communicate and share information.

The Go Zone

Acceptance

The "Go Zone" is when everyone is truly on board and ready to go. If people have enough time and are given some help in working through the previous stages, they eventually come to a feeling of *acceptance* with a certain degree of expectation. Implementing some "rites of passage" at this point can be beneficial as a way to provide closure of the past and momentum toward the future. For example, one company took a prototype printer to the parking lot and allowed people to take turns whacking it with a sledgehammer. Another held a pizza party in an empty production facility before it was refitted for new office space. A third took a photo of the "old gang" and put the image on coffee mugs inscribed with "RIP" – rest in peace.

Some people never reach the necessary stage of acceptance. They fight to the end and struggle with every step. It is imperative that those people who have been sitting on the fence, and unwilling or unable to get enrolled in the change, either get on board or get out. You and your sponsor must take determinative action or risk undermining the commitment of those who have already come to accept change. Expectations must be made clear, time limits must be set and corrective action, including termination, must be taken if necessary. Acutely resistive people need to understand: "This is what I need for you to do to support the change – this is what will happen if you do not."

Excitement, Clarity and Implementation

In the Go Zone you have the ship pointed North, the winds at your back and all hands on deck. People have become excited about the possibilities and are clear about their place in the paradigm. Now is the time to establish action items and cross-functional teams. Now is the time for technology implementation and project management. Now is the time for communication, collaboration and clarity of expectations.

People will go through this cycle at varying rates and their reactions will be dynamic – not a steady progression. They may skip certain emotional experiences or linger longer in some more than others. If you recognize and understand the emotional implications of change, as well as the technological hurdles that must be overcome, you will be more likely to bring about meaningful and beneficial change with your document strategy.

To assist you in the Go Zone:

- Take action on issues within your area of control.
- Let go of what you cannot control.
- Visualize yourself (positively) in the new paradigm.

To assist others in the Go Zone:

- Clarify purpose and desired outcomes (again).
- Involve the people affected by the change in planning and implementation.
- Celebrate small successes; publicly recognize new ideas and how they have been implemented.
- Provide ongoing feedback, training and information.

Corporate Culture Affects your Strategy

The culture of your organization can either support your document strategy or work against it as a significant barrier. All organizations have a subjective or invisible culture that will influence your success or failure. You may have a culture that stops the forward progress of a change initiative while the same initiative in another company is implemented quite easily. Experts estimate that between fifty and seventy percent of all reengineering efforts fail, often because a culture does not accept new approaches. [12] You must prepare for and accept the fact that the culture of your organization has a significant and potentially negative influence on your ability to implement your strategy.

While a set of engineering drawings or system schematics adequately depicts the performance of a piece of equipment, the performance of a company is rarely encapsulated in its organizational charts, strategic plans or mission statement. The difference is the affect of corporate culture on the way things actually get done. Your firm's culture can be of great assistance to you if it is receptive to new ideas and adept with change. But if your culture prevents your company from accepting change – essentially holding the company hostage – then your efforts to implement your document strategy will be severely inhibited if not repressed altogether.

Corporate culture provides the human glue that can rally the collective energy of your company toward improvements and accomplishments, or it can be the glue that fastens your organization to "the way things have always been." Like the personality of a person, the culture of an organization is not something that is readily apparent at first glance. But after you get to know it, you begin to see the shared beliefs and unwritten ground rules that determine the ways in which your organization and its people behave.

What Kind of Culture do you have?

It is important to understand your current culture, its strengths and style, and its potential to either help or hinder your efforts. One of the biggest challenges in trying to understand your own culture is that it is difficult for an insider to see. Overcome this by observing your organization as if you were an outsider. Here are a number of clues: [13]

- **What gets attention** in conversations and in meetings? If, for example, 90 percent of a typical meeting is spent talking about reducing costs, and 10 percent is spent on how the customers are feeling, then you probably have more of a cost-driven than a customer-driven culture.

- **Notice people's behavior.** Make a list of behaviors that you see every day. Do the behaviors you observe contribute to or detract from your efforts?

- **Look at your policies and procedures.** If you have shelves of policy manuals that describe in detail how people must perform the duties of their job and how they must conduct themselves at work, then chances are that your culture is one where people tend to follow the rules and avoid risk. If you have only a few casual guidelines written up in one manual, your culture may be more entrepreneurial with lots of new ideas and free flowing communication.

- **What are the "hero stories?"** The behaviors and actions that become legend within your company are strong indicators of your culture. Who do people talk about with pride and respect? Who gets rousing applause at meetings? What are the behaviors that warrant that applause? Hero stories model the behavior of employees that is expected by your corporate culture.

- **Get feedback.** Ask employees (especially new employees) to describe the culture and personality of your company or department.

Characteristics of a High Performance Culture

While you cannot really see your corporate culture, you can observe the behavior or actions of people that set the norms for your organization. Every company is different and has both positive and negative characteristics. Even companies of similar size in the same industry will have different cultures, just as twins who grow up in the same household can be very different.

There is no perfect culture, but the following chart summarizes some of the characteristics found in high performing organizations.[14] Organizations that embrace, adopt and implement change easily generally exhibit these high performance characteristics, while those that perform less admirably experience the corresponding cultural barriers to change.

High Performance Characteristics	Cultural Barriers
Empowered people and cross-functional communication.	Turf-building and hierarchical organizational structures.
Open, honest and flowing communication.	Hidden agendas, dishonesty, lack of openness.
Trust and confidence.	Distrust and fear.
Long-term, quality, service and excellence.	Short-term, strictly bottom-line.
Customer-oriented, externally focused.	Task-oriented, internally focused.
"Can-do" spirit.	"Cannot be done" attitude.
Personal responsibility.	Blame and making excuses.
Embracing new ideas.	Prejudiced and judgmental.
Innovation, ingenuity, breakthroughs.	Holding on to the past, resistance to change.
Flexible, fluid and rapidly responsive.	Strict rules and rigid policies.
Win/Win.	Win/Lose.

Tips for Combating the Negative Aspects of Culture

What can you do if your corporate culture does not exhibit the high performance characteristics listed above? Here are a few principles that will help you overcome a less-than-high performing culture: [15]

- **Practice what you preach.** You must model the behavior you wish were present in other people. Any change to corporate culture must start with key leaders, and as a document strategist you are a leader regardless of your rank or position. People will look to you as a role model and a guide to follow. Your commitment and leadership will directly influence whether or not the rest of the organization will follow.

- **Reinforce new and positive behaviors.** The practice of catching people doing the right things is a key to overcoming bad cultural habits. Provide reinforcing feedback on a day-to-day basis and build into your strategy a system for people to offer feedback to others.

- **Repetition, repetition, repetition.** You must reiterate the message of your document strategy over and over. The frequently used term *document strategy evangelist* comes to mind. If you preach the virtues of your plan with simplicity, consistency and repetition, you will eventually get through to people. Changing aspects of your corporate culture requires a steady continuum that finally reaches a critical mass.

- **Consistency.** You do not want people within your organization to consider your document strategy as just another "gimmick of the month." If they do, you can be assured your plan will soon be a thing of the past. Your evangelist message must be the same month after month, and, if needed, year after year. While some of the aspects of your strategy will, and must, be revised as you progress, the essential message concerning how documents, technology and people need to perform should stay the same.

- **Passion**. You must believe in your strategy and feel passionate about it, or no one else will. You must communicate your enthusiasm and passion to the rest of the organization at every opportunity. You must pay nearly obsessive attention to sharing your passion with the people who must adopt and support your strategy.

Change Cultural History

You may need to alter *cultural history* in order to enact your document strategy. If the history in your organization is a legacy of resistance to change, slow progress toward improvements and the avoidance of risk, you may need to change the norm of how things typically get done. One way to overcome negative cultural history is by both acknowledging it and denying it. Take a rebellious stance against the cultural dysfunction that prevents improvement from happening successfully.

If your company has difficulty actually implementing improvements, or often fails to complete process reengineering efforts, turn things around by building a reputation that says: "We *always* implement!" With this as your mantra, live up to your promise by selecting solutions that can be successfully implemented…and implement them. Build your reputation as a person or department who can implement a beneficial change and make it stick. People will begin to say: "Those guys always implement!" By demonstrating consistent success in the face of resistance you will begin to change cultural history.

If you become known for your ability to change things for the better, people will become excited about working with you and supporting your strategy. This is another instance where your earlier work will pay off. Perhaps your cultural history is one where improvements are not implemented because there has not been a clear understanding of what needed to be changed in the first place and why. People struggle, become frustrated and quit because they do not recognize problems and hindrances ahead of time. As mentioned before, the effort you put into assessment, evaluation and planning falls into the "pay now or pay later" category. If you have followed the process outlined in earlier chapters, you've paid your dues. People may resist and disparage your efforts, but if you have done your homework you are in a position to minimize or remove the barriers to your success and rewrite cultural history.

Questions to Consider

- What are the financial methods and hard numbers you will use to demonstrate return on investment and justify your strategy?

- How will you demonstrate to your co-workers that your strategy will benefit them?

- What are the likely reactions that people will have to the changes proposed in your strategy?

- How will you minimize the negative affects of their reactions to change?

- What kind of culture is present in your organization? What aspects will either help or hinder your strategy?

7

Project Planning and Implementation

Even the most thoughtful and comprehensive strategy will not be successful if it is not executed effectively. All of your assessments, conclusions and proposed actions now must come together in a project plan that maps the course of your strategy and directs your efforts successfully. Many aspects of your document strategy may be similar to those put into practice at another company, but the details of its implementation will be unique to your particular organization. This makes it difficult to follow a generic implementation formula. Only you can anticipate and adjust the exact route you must take. While the methods and principles of project management are wide-ranging,[1] this element of the Document Strategy Model explores some universal techniques that will make launching your strategy much easier and aid successful implementation.

Develop a Project Plan

A project plan is essential to organize the actions of your document strategy so that they will be clearly understood by everyone involved. A good project plan outlines who will do what and when, and allows you to monitor your project and keep everyone on track. Without a project plan, you cannot measure your progress and results against your objectives.

Developing a project plan is like contracting. It holds your sponsor accountable for providing the support you need and ensures that change enablers perform as they have promised. You will be held accountable as well – accountable to repay your sponsor with results. For this reason, be sure that your project plan is realistic. Be careful what you commit to. It is easy to become excited about the possibilities, but do not commit to more than you can deliver when the time comes. It is better to renegotiate your deliverables than to fail to deliver.

Framework of a Project Plan

Your document strategy will most likely include a series of related projects. You will need a project plan for each. View each individual project as a combination of activities aimed at achieving specific outcomes. Those outcomes represent your overall strategic results. The way you organize the activities and responsibilities associated with each project will ultimately determine how productive and successful your document strategy is. Use the following framework to organize your project:

- Compose a Project Statement
- Define Project Objectives
- Challenge Assumptions and Verify Facts
- Construct an Action Plan
- Assess your Action Plan
- Pilot, Test and Evaluate
- Implement Improvements and Solutions
- Demonstrate your Success
- Turn over to Sustaining Sponsors

Your earlier work will serve you well when putting together your project plan. You have already collected the information you need, defined the specific problems to overcome and determined the desired state for improvement. You have selected solutions and established financial data to justify your actions. Now you must challenge your assumptions, verify your facts and outline the action items that need to be completed.

Compose a Project Statement

A project statement describes your project's purpose. It establishes a specific destination while you map the rest of your journey. Consider the following project statement: *"Standardize document composition software."* While this statement appears to be concise, it can mean very different things to different people. For example:

- What does "standardize" mean? (Purchase? Install? Test? Train?)
- What will the new software be?
- When will it be introduced?
- How much can be spent (money, time, effort) to standardize the software?

A project statement must clearly describe your overall purpose, the time frames associated with your project and the resources needed to put it into place. It should contain the following basic elements:

Elements of a Project Statement

Element	Example
Action Word	Implement
End Result	New document composition software at all production sites
Target Completion Date	By April 15, 2001
Cost Guideline	At a cost not to exceed $75,000

The original project statement might now read: *"Implement new document composition software at all production sites by April 15, 2001 at a cost not to exceed $75,000."*

You must establish your project's purpose in a manner that is clearly and easily understood. If your project seems vague, the people who are sponsors, enablers and targets of your change will be much less likely to perform in ways that will bring your project to a successful completion. Use the elements above as a basis for your project statement, and adjust and adapt the specifics to accommodate your particular situation.

Define Project Objectives

Project objectives are statements that describe the conditions that will exist when your project is completed. Work with your sponsor and the various people who will implement and enable the changes needed to develop your specific objectives. This way everyone involved will be able to gauge how well the project is doing. One way to determine project objectives is to answer the following question: "This project will be a success when (if, by, etc)...." For example:

- This project will be a success when we install and test the software in our production facilities in Seattle, Portland, Salt Lake City and Boise.

- This project will be a success when all production sites are functional by April 15th.

- This project will be a success if our costs of implementation are less than $75,000.

It is important to provide a focus for your project by defining objectives that are clearly and easily measured. Clear objectives enable everyone to know exactly what results are expected and to focus their performance to meet those goals. You will be able to lead your project effectively and efficiently. Leading a project and providing meaningful coaching is difficult unless you have mutually established expectations. Project objectives help everyone recognize when things are drifting off course and point the way to the necessary course corrections.

The benefit of having clear project objectives is that everyone's

> **When setting objectives for your project, make sure that they pass the "SMART" test.**
>
> **S = Specific**
> Do your objectives convey the same meaning to you, your sponsor, your team members and anyone else who reads it?
>
> **M = Measurable**
> Are your objectives described in tangible and measurable terms? Are the results verifiable?
>
> **A = Agreed Upon**
> Have your sponsors and team members agreed upon your objectives?
>
> **R = Realistic**
> Are your objectives both challenging and realistic? Can the goals actually be achieved?
>
> **T = Time-bounded**
> Do your objectives have a deadline or time interval as a means of monitoring your progress and the progress of others?

responsibilities are defined – nothing is assumed or left out. Team members will be better able to appraise their own effectiveness because the progress of your project is apparent at all times. You will provide a sense of purpose. Everyone involved will have a more positive attitude toward your project and be excited about achieving common goals. In addition, project objectives provide a set of expectations and a clear direction for newly-added team members to follow.

Sample list of project objectives:

1. As a result of this project, one document composition tool will be used, saving $10,000 per year on maintenance of other systems by April 15, 2001.

2. As a result of this project, users will be able to share documents and information more easily, increasing productivity across the various site locations by 10% by the end of the third quarter of 2001.

3. As a result of this project, the number of document

composition programs will be reduced to one, saving approximately $8,500 in ongoing training for other software by April 15, 2001.

4. As a result of this project, documents will now be available in each site (Seattle, Portland, Salt Lake City and Boise), resulting in a reduction of re-work and duplication. Estimated labor savings are $52,000 per year beginning approximately April 15, 2001.

Challenge Assumptions and Verify Facts

Before you layout the specific tasks and timing of your project, it is imperative that you challenge your assumptions and verify your facts. Mistakes or omissions may have been made during your information gathering efforts and conditions may have changed since you first conducted your assessments. By challenging your assumptions and verifying facts, you will confirm the information you are using as a basis for your project is accurate and that everyone is working from the "same page." Do this by creating a list of your assumptions and facts like so:

Assumptions	**Facts**
90% of workstations will not require hardware upgrades to run the new software.	Site license will be obtained to lower the total cost of the software.
Software support will be provided internally; expertise will be built into current staff.	Upgrades will be handled by the document services staff.
Document templates will be created to standardize the look of corporate documents.	Documents one year old or newer will be translated. All others will be converted as needed.
Production printers will not need to beupgraded for the new software to work.	Updated fonts will be installed at the time the software is installed.

To challenge your assumptions and verify facts, ask questions like:

- Are your assumptions correct?

- Have conditions changed in a way that will affect your assumptions?

- Will your assumptions affect other aspects that you have not considered?

- What happens if your assumptions prove to be inaccurate? Do you have a contingency plan?

- Have you verified that your facts are correct?

- Do you have firm commitments in writing?

It is also helpful to explore the factors that will either help or hinder the implementation of your project. What elements can you rely on to ease your way toward implementation? What are the elements that will, despite your better efforts, block your forward progress and must be either avoided or overcome? By investigating these factors beforehand, you will be better able to anticipate and minimize the effects of the barriers that exist and maximize the conditions that will help you toward a successful conclusion. Some of the questions to consider are:

- **Will the technological landscape change in ways that will assist or block your progress?** Technology evolves for a number of reasons, new standards are introduced, de facto computer platforms change, vendors merge, etc. Expect that technology will evolve quickly and may either present new opportunities or render your approach obsolete.

- **Have people realized that your strategy is here to stay?** It can take time (sometimes several months) for people to fully accept your strategy. Eventually people who have been somewhat resistant or ambivalent will realize, "Gee, this isn't going away."

- **Are people motivated and enthusiastic, or simply doing as they are told?** This can depend on whether people are assigned to your project or

have volunteered. Another factor is whether or
not they are given the appropriate amount of time
to work on your project in addition to their day-to-
day duties.

- **Are people qualified?** Highly competent and
  qualified individuals are essential for your project
  to succeed. Some people who volunteer (or get
  volunteered) may not be qualified, however. For
  example, a person assigned to your project may
  delegate it to someone else on his or her staff.
  If this person is not prepared, or does not have
  the skills you need, your project will suffer. You
  may need to renegotiate this assignment with your
  sponsor.

- **Have adequate resources been dedicated?** People
  may be well intentioned, but if there is a shortage
  of time, technology or other resources it can be
  very difficult for people to feel enthusiastic about
  your project.

- **Will people be evaluated and rewarded for their
  participation in your strategy?** If people are
  compensated only on their "regular" job, your
  project will take a back seat. When possible,
  link the involvement of people in your strategy
  with their individual performance goals and job
  evaluations. Negotiate special compensation with
  your sponsor.

Construct an Action Plan

An action plan is a list of all the tasks that need to be
performed in order to complete your project. Each task must
be relevant to your project goals, be specific yet adaptable, and
sequenced in time. To construct your action plan, assign tasks
to individuals and teams, then outline the timing of when each
task must be completed. You will avoid omitting critical tasks
and provide a foundation upon which schedules, resources and
budgets can be planned, executed, monitored and evaluated.

An action plan is essential because it establishes how the work
associated with your project will be performed. Involving

other project team members will promote their input and commitment. All major events and due dates in your action plan must be clearly outlined and the exact sequence of work and interrelationships should be identified.

When constructing your action plan, ask questions like:

- What major tasks must be accomplished to complete your project?
- When must these tasks be completed?
- Who should be responsible to accomplish each task?
- How much time can be spent to finish each task?
- What, specifically, will be required from each assignment?

Interrelationships of Project Tasks

Dependent tasks

In some cases, the completion of one task depends on the completion of another. For example, you cannot install software until hardware is in place. It is important to understand the interrelationships of project tasks to determine how changes or problems with one task will affect your overall effort. You must determine if individual tasks must be performed in sequential order or can be performed as parallel activities. Your project will be more efficient if you compare these dependencies and select a sequence that will make the best use of your available time.

Tasks also can depend on the person conducting them (e.g., Paul is the only one who can do the installation). In this case, the tasks cannot be performed in parallel because only one person has the expertise or the time to complete the task. Use the following steps when assessing the interrelationships of project tasks.

1. List tasks by chronological date to see an overview of your project flow.

2. List tasks by function to understand interrelationships of tasks.

3. Determine which tasks are dependent and sequential and which tasks are independent.

4. Determine the tasks that only one person or department can perform.

5. Consider the amount of time available for team members to work on task.

6. Consider calendar issues like plant shutdowns, vacations, etc.

Parallel tasks

When possible, schedule independent tasks to occur simultaneously. You will reduce your total project duration by performing tasks in parallel. You may also, however, increase your risks and incremental costs. Weigh your options and choose the best approach for your particular situation.

Lead- and Lag-Time

You may need to specify lead- or lag-time between tasks. In a *finish-to-start* relationship, an overlap between tasks is called lead-time. This is because the start of the task precedes, or leads, the finish of its predecessor. For example, you may want to start installing software when only half of the computer workstations have been installed. In a *finish-to-start* relationship, a gap or delay between tasks is called lag-time. For example, you may want to start testing your software only after all of the workstations are up.

Methods and Tools for Scheduling Tasks

If your project is detailed and complicated, you may find it helpful to use a software program like Microsoft Project to construct your action plan. [2] These programs use a Gantt chart [3] to represent how your project is structured. A Gantt chart is a horizontal bar chart that graphically displays the time relationships between the different tasks.

Case Example: XYZ Laboratories Action Plan

XYZ has constructed the following action plan to facilitate the installation of new document composition software in their various production sites. Lisa Ness, the project manager, has included a project statement along with a list of tasks that must be performed to complete the project. Each task is assigned to an individual or group, and start and end dates have been agreed upon. Dependent tasks are noted at the right when applicable. Note that lag- and lead-times have been incorporated into the start and end dates, and tasks that can be done in parallel have been indicated at the right.

Action Plan

Project Statement: Implement new document composition software at all production sites by April 15, 2001 at a cost not to exceed $75,000

Project Manager: Lisa Ness   **Date:** February 12, 2001

Task	Who	Start	End	Dependent Task
Install software at production sites	Paul	2/11	2/24	None
Test printer connection & file structures	Paul & Doc Svc Staff	2/22	2/23	Software install (parallel tasks)
Create custom files & templates	Allyson	3/1	3/15	Install & testing
Test document Templates	Doc Svc Staff	3/16	3/22	Create custom templates
Pilot document composition & printing	Doc Svc Staff	3/20	4/1	Test templates (parallel tasks)
Verify document quality	Allyson & Doc Svc Staff	3/22	4/10	Pilot document composition (parallel tasks)
Use software for production	Doc Svc Staff	4/10	4/15	Troubleshooting unexpected problems

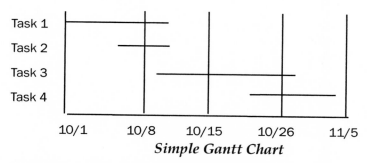

Simple Gantt Chart

Project management software will allow you to view and modify your project tasks, milestones and critical paths by time frame and activity. Some people find these tools to be indispensable while others find that they make things more complicated. Use whatever method makes the most sense for your particular project.

Assess Your Action Plan

No matter how thoroughly you have constructed your action plan, you cannot anticipate all the outcomes and risks. You can minimize this uncertainty by assessing your action plan before putting it into place. Reconsider and rehearse all the plan's actions. View your planning as an evolutionary process. As you implement your plan, you may discover and generate new information, so it is important to continually reassess and revise your actions. You may also find that action planning will help clarify your original assessments and goals. Here are some questions to help assess your plan: [4]

- **Are you clear about your long- and short-term project objectives?** Consider the axiom: *Envision long and plan short.* Be specific about the early steps in your plan and more flexible about the later ones. This will help keep you pointed in the right direction and allow you to make the necessary course corrections along the way.

- **Is your action plan consistent with your earlier assessments?** Consider whether the key assumptions underlying your action plan are consistent and valid. Be careful that the information you are relying on is based on facts, not inference, implication or speculation.

- **Is your plan feasible given known constraints and opportunities?** Pay particular attention to timing and workload.

- **Is your action plan realistic given your ability to exercise authority and influence?** If you do not have the full and consistent support of your sponsor, you may be in a position of "over-functioning" as a change agent. You may not have the authority to direct the people you need to participate in your project or the ability to influence the conditions that inhibit your effort.

- **What is the likely impact of your action plan?** Will it be effective for you? Will it be effective for your organization and your constituents? Have you thought not only about those who will be directly affected by your plan, but also about those who may be indirectly affected? Be cognizant of the trade-offs you are making, if any, and understand the risks involved for you and for those who might be impacted by your plan.

- **Have you examined the urgency and sequence of the tasks in your plan?** Be sure to differentiate between urgent and important problems and opportunities. Design your action plan with incremental steps so that you can "test the waters" whenever possible.

- **Have you made sure that early action steps do not unnecessarily or prematurely rule out future alternatives?** Consider the horizon. Take into account that as you move forward with your action plan the climate and conditions in which you operate will most likely change.

- **Have you put in place a process to ensure that you will periodically reevaluate and, if appropriate, modify your action plan?** It is very easy to get caught up in the "action" and lose sight of your objectives. Take the time to reflect on and learn from your experiences as you go. It is as important to learn from your successes as it is to learn from your failures.

Determine Risks and Develop Contingencies

When planning a project, it is imperative that you consider the likelihood that your project will be successful. What is the probability of success for each step of your action plan? If you can determine the risks associated with your plan and take into account the contingencies ("what if?") you will be better able to plan for them ahead of time. This is especially important for the most critical steps in your action plan. If the probability of success for a given action step is low, you must develop other alternatives. Do this by compiling a list of questions to assess your risks, and then answering them honestly. Some questions to consider are: [5]

- Is this a new technology?
- Has this been done before?
- Will conditions change while you are implementing your project?
- What will be the outcome if things go wrong?
- If things go wrong, what will you do?
- What is the probability that your project will be successful? (100%? 50%? 10%?)

Unless you are 100 percent certain that your project will be successful and will not encounter unanticipated problems along the way, you must develop contingencies and corrective steps for the risks you anticipate. A contingency plan will minimize your risk, and give you room to stay on schedule and meet your objectives. It will allow you to react quickly and confidently to problems that occur. Your backup plans should answer the question: "If things go wrong because of..."

Levels of risk and uncertainty vary from project to project. The more complex your project is, the more likely that you will need to "hedge" against the following factors:

Estimates   The best estimates are based on historical data, but predicting the future is far from certain. Complete information is often unavailable. Estimates are not always accurate and may contain errors in financial and technical data.

Design changes Highly complex tasks and projects may require adjustments along the way. External and internal situations may change over time.

Omissions Sometimes information is forgotten or overlooked. Information that was not important in the initial stages may be important in later stages.

When making a contingency plan, your goal is to prevent your project from going off course. You will also enrich your entire project planning process by thinking through some alternative routes. Follow these steps to develop a contingency plan:

1. Review your objectives and your action steps. Consider potential problems.

2. Assess the probability that any given problem will occur (e.g., "There is a 50% chance it will occur.").

3. Determine the likely impacts of potential problems (e.g., "What might happen as a result of this?").

4. List your options and alternatives. What are the various ways each risk or problem can be minimized or solved?

5. Develop actions you will take to prevent the potential problem from occurring. If a problem cannot be avoided, develop a contingency or countermeasure.

Pilot, Test and Evaluate

In addition to thoughtful planning, successful projects require thoughtful implementation. Do this by piloting your plans on a small scale and monitoring the results whenever possible. In essence, a pilot is an experiment to evaluate a proposed solution. It provides objective data that you can use to decide whether or not to move forward with your action plan.

During this trial run, collect information on your key process measures and compare it to your previously collected measurement data. The evidence will either support your plan or indicate you need to come up with new ideas and solutions. Do the results you observe provide the outcomes you anticipate? If not, why? You can be more confident that your project will be a success if the results of your pilot implementation are successful. Conduct your pilot by following these three steps:

1. Pilot the improvement ideas.

2. Measure the pilot against current state.

3. Implement only after pilot improvements are proven and measurable.

You may have succeeded in improving the process or solving the problem, but you will not know for certain if you are successful until you gather all the available data and evaluate it. Has your plan actually helped improve the current situation? Are any further problems or opportunities present? Do the results of your pilot indicate that you should move forward with full implementation or return to the drawing board? Often, a proposed solution must be modified or scrapped. Evaluate new solutions and plans by conducting another pilot until you can confirm that your efforts have been successful.

Implement Improvements and Solutions

Once you have refined your plans so they meet your project goals, you need to implement and standardize the new process. Some of the steps to follow are:

1. Document the improved process via procedures and operating guidelines.

2. Conduct training on the new process.

3. Gather and provide ongoing feedback to, and from, the people involved.

4. Assure the delivery of promised improvements.

In this stage, your solutions and improvements become an ordinary part of the ongoing process. It is important that you document how the newly improved process must be performed, what technology and systems must be used, and who is responsible to carry out the various duties of the process. Orient people to the new process by providing training and procedures, and share those procedures with supervisors and managers. Offer coaching and feedback.

During implementation, be aware of any last minute hitches or problems. The approach of "we'll fix it later" rarely works, so be sure that any technological glitches are addressed promptly and correctly.

Assess Project Success

Once your project has been implemented, evaluate the performance of the process or solution to ensure that the improvements you anticipated and promised are actually delivered. This requires careful examination. You may be tempted to skip this step and simply declare success and move on. But assessing and demonstrating your success is essential in order to build your reputation for achievement and encourage sponsors and co-workers to embrace and accept your document strategy efforts in the future. Questions to consider are:

- Did you achieve the outcomes you set for this project? To what extent?
- Did the project end within budget?
- Were costs planned and allocated appropriately?
- Was the return on investment that you anticipated achieved?
- Were areas of opportunities identified and responded to?
- Did the project start and end on time?
- Were problems handled promptly and efficiently?
- Were all of the tasks complete? Were they correctly performed and on time?

- Were the correct resources deployed for this project?

- Did team members have the tools and time they needed to perform their assignments?

- Were resources realistically established in light of the budget or time estimates of the project?

Demonstrate Your Success

Once you have achieved success, demonstrate it. Communicate the benefit of your efforts to your sponsors and co-workers. By doing so, you will be more likely to win continuing support and justification for similar document strategy projects. Do this by preparing a written report for your sponsors. In addition, it is helpful to prepare a condensed version for your team members and others who may offer "testimony" to your success. Follow your initial project plan and describe the results of your project. Your report should include the following components:

- Project Timeline. Indicate the beginning and ending date of your project. Also note whether your project was completed on time or if it took longer than anticipated. If you were on schedule, list the aspects that helped you meet your timeline. If you were off schedule, list the causes anδ the methods you used to correct the timeline.

- Project Benefits and Outcomes. List and describe the results of your project and how they were measured. Describe the benefits you achieved and detail the hard numbers. Compare and contrast the outcomes to your original objectives.

- Continuing Opportunities. Describe the other opportunities that resulted from your project.

- Financial Outcomes. Describe both the estimated and actual costs of your project. Be sure to include clear and quantifiable financial figures. If you came in under budget, indicate the reasons why and how these savings can be applied in other areas. If you went over budget, indicate the reasons why and how the deficit may be recovered elsewhere.

- Suggested Follow Up. Recommend how the results of your project can be sustained or updated.

- Lessons Learned. Describe what you learned from your experience. How can your success be duplicated? How can mistakes or mishaps be avoided in the future? Describe what worked well, and what must be done differently in future projects.

- Project Team Recognition. Indicate the team members who made key contributions. Suggest ways to recognize, compensate and celebrate their success. If people feel that their work is appreciated, they will be more likely to willingly support and participate in future document strategy efforts.

- Additional Comments. Offer additional comments or concerns that will be helpful for evaluating the success of your project. Opportunities for continuous improvement should be recapped as well.

Turn Over to Sustaining Sponsors

Even though your project is completed, your job is not over. You must turn over the improved process to a sustaining sponsor. A sustaining sponsor (or sponsors) must assume the responsibility to make certain that the process continues to perform as it should, and recommend and implement changes and adjustments over time. After all, if your project is a success, it is likely that you will be working on further document strategy initiatives and you will not have time to ensure the longevity of your improvements. How well you orchestrate your project's ongoing success is also a sign of effective project management. You must determine what long-term "care and feeding" is needed to foster the continued prosperity of your project and bestow that responsibility on a sustaining sponsor.

Questions to Consider:

- What statement best describes the purpose of your project?

- What are the specific objectives of your project?

- Do you have a list of the assumptions and facts associated with your project? Are they accurate and verifiable?

- Do you have an action plan in place that outlines the tasks that must be performed and assigns timelines and responsibilities for these activities?

- Have you assessed the risks associated with your project and the likelihood that it will be successful?

- How will you pilot your project and evaluate the results?

- How will you demonstrate your success once your project has been implemented?

- Who must take over the improved process and ensure that the solutions you have put into place continue to bear fruit?

8

The Navigator

Perhaps the most famous explorer is Christopher Columbus. It's nearly impossible to exaggerate the historical significance of Columbus. As school kids we learned that not only did Columbus discover America, but he also proved that the Earth is round, not flat. While the details of these attributions can be debated, history has forever bestowed Columbus with iconic significance as a great thinker and explorer. And rightly so, his legacy has been nothing less than global in its impact. Columbus ushered in a new age, and the world was never the same. As one who led the way, Columbus deserves recognition for sparking the intellectual transformation that became known as the "Age of Discovery."

While your document strategy may not change civilization forever, you often will feel that you are launching forth into a strange new territory. As you travel these unfamiliar waters, ponder the lessons you can learn from this greatest of navigators and explorers.

Born in Genoa, Italy, in 1451, Columbus was among the first to explore the uncharted seas to the West. In the 15th century, celestial navigation was a highly developed discipline, and the favored method of sailing under unfamiliar stars. Compasses, astrolabes, sextants and hourglasses were important navigational aids. Columbus had all of these devices on board with him during his famous voyages. He was well-schooled in the science and technology of celestial navigation, but Columbus relied instead on "dead reckoning" to determine his ships positions. This meant that he used his experience, observations, intuition and guesswork to navigate. He trusted his naked eye observations more than any device. Use these skills of navigation to chart the course of your document strategy.

Columbus was masterful at reading the signs of nature - the behavior of birds, the smell of the air, the condition of the seas - but what set Columbus apart from other navigators of his time was his remarkable ability to gather information and combine that with his real life experiences. He balanced the often-conflicting maps and charts of the day with his practical knowledge, but more than that, Columbus drew upon the science and knowledge accumulated over millennia - Ptolemy, Toscanelli, Marco Polo - in a way that few navigators were able to do. Collect information, read the signs and map your strategy with a broad perspective.

Columbus questioned the traditional view of the world. Since antiquity, philosophers and scientists had speculated that the Earth was round. Columbus agreed with these heretical theories because they matched his real-world experiences. He was certain that he could reach the Far East by sailing west - only the distance was in dispute.

Few people believed Columbus was right. Despite having a completed plan for sailing to the Indies, it took nearly nine years - from 1484 until that famous year of 1492 - for the explorer to win the sponsorship he needed. Royal patrons throughout Europe rejected his proposal on the grounds that it was too expensive, that Columbus was only a "visionary," and that he was wrong about the measurements. And after all, there were only "worthless rocky points" for land to the West. With his hope nearly gone, Columbus made a final appeal to King Ferdinand and Queen Isabella of Spain, who begrudgingly agreed to sponsor his expedition. In April of 1492, Columbus departed on his voyage, and the rest is history. As ships returned to their ports from newly-found lands and oceans, a new picture of the world emerged - a picture based on empirical evidence, not on theory, tradition or assumption. Be confident that beyond the horizon waits a world of success for your document strategy.

Advances in nautical navigation typified the Age of Discovery, but it was this psychology of discovery - the courage and inspiration to look beyond traditional boundaries - that rewarded those daring enough to venture out in search of riches. New views resulted in new maps for discovery.

Advances in computer technology typify the Information Age, but it is the same psychology of discovery - the courage and inspiration to design a document strategy - that will reward those daring enough to venture out in search of success. You are the thinker and explorer that will lead the way to discovery. Be the first to explore uncharted seas. Map the course of your document strategy to new worlds of improvement and profit.

Like Columbus, you may find that sponsorship and support are hard to come by. Few decision-makers will see documents as little more than "worthless rocky points." But as the story of Columbus teaches, if you apply practical knowledge mixed with the skills of a navigator, you will eventually convince your patrons of the validity of your document strategy.

The Age of Discovery was motivated not by a desire to discover New Worlds, but by a need to find new routes to Old World marketplaces. Whether your document strategy is intended to improve existing business practices or designed to uncover new passages to new markets, you must navigate your journey like Columbus. Use your experience, observations and assessments to chart your course. Utilize the technology of the day, but trust your naked eye observations more. Use this book to gather information, question the traditional view of the world and pilot your strategy with a broad perspective.

History will certainly record the Information Age as an era

marked by escalating developments in technology. The real discoveries, however, may be found by explorers intrepid enough to navigate beyond the traditional boundaries of the Document.

Bon Voyage.

Notes:

Chapter One

1. According to research done by Coopers and Lybrand. As quoted in a correspondence sent to author on October 12, 1997.

2. According to research done by Cap Ventures. As quoted by: Barb Pellow and Carrie Griffin, *Print On Demand Business,* September 1998, p. 27. Note: the Gartner Group also found a similar statistic. Statistics of this kind are frequently quoted in various industry journals and at conferences, and can often be attributed to more than one source.

3. According to research done by the Gartner Group. As quoted by: Mitchell Gross, "Building the Electronic Warehouse," *Imaging World,* January 1997.

4. Tony McKinley, "Managing All Information Assets," *Document Management,* August 1997, p. 14.

5. Pellow and Griffin, *Print On Demand Business.*

6. The actual dawn of human civilization is somewhat arbitrary. The hieroglyphs discovered at the Giza plateau near Cairo, Egypt have been dated back four millennia (c. 2300BC), but the content is thought to have originated much earlier (c. 3300BC). It is believed that the "pyramid texts" in the Unas pyramid are the oldest religious

documents in the world and significantly pre-date the more famous Dead Sea scrolls (c. 100BC). Unas was the last king of the fifth Egyptian dynasty. See: Robert Bauval and Adrian Gilbert, *The Orion Mystery* (Three Rivers Press, 1995), pp. 57-69.

7. Richard Saul Wurman, *Information Anxiety* (Out of print). As quoted by: G.A. Marken, *Document Management*, May 1997, p. 30.

8. Gross, "Building the Electronic Warehouse," *Imaging World*.

9. Peter Drucker. From his keynote address at Sequent Computer's enterprise solutions summit, January 1999.

10. P.A. David, "Computer and Dynamo: Discussion Paper #172," Stanford Center for Economic Policy Research, Stanford University, 1991.

11. According to M. Khosrow-Pour, professor of information systems, Pennsylvania State University, in correspondence sent to the author on June 21, 1999.

12. Louis Zacharilla, "The Future of Output," *Document Processing Technology,* January 1998, p. 18.

13. Keith Davidson. From his keynote address at the Xplor International Document Strategies Conference, February 1998.

14. Gross, "Building the Electronic Warehouse," *Imaging World*.

15. According to Khosrow-Pour, June 21, 1999.

16. Robert Kunio, "E-Pioneers," *e-bill*, October 1999, p. 16.

17. *National Geographic*, May 1998.

18. See: Peter M. Senge, *The Fifth Discipline: The Art and Practice of the Learning Organization* (Doubleday, 1994).

19. Adapted from: Michael Turton, "Aligning Corporate, IT and Document Strategies," *Document Processing Technology,* June 1999, pp. 12 – 14. Dr. Turton is with Cavendish Consultants, a U.K. firm specializing in document design and strategies.

20. Michael Zeis, et al., *The 1998 Xplor International Technology Directions Survey*, p. 27.

Chapter Three

1. Interview with author, February 1998. Xplor International is the Electronic Document Systems Association. See: www.xplor.org.

2. Interview with author, February 1998. Warner-Lambert is a *Fortune 500* company that is best known as a leader in the pharmaceutical industry.

3. Interview with author, February 1998.

4. Interview with author, April 1998. P.C. (Pat) McGrew and partner W.D. (Bill) McDaniel founded GenText, a successful technology start-up, before founding the McGrew+McDaniel Group. They have also co-authored two books for McGraw-Hill: *In-House Publishing in a Mainframe Environment* and *Online Text Management.*

5. Interview with author, March 2000. In addition to her position at Oregon Graduate Institute of Science and Technology, Smid works as an organizational effectiveness consultant for IBM (Sequent Computers).

6. Adapted from: David P. Hanna, *Designing Organizations for High Performance* (Addison-Wesley, 1988), pp. 38-68.

7. Bruno Giussani, "Eruobytes," *New York Times Online,* February 3, 1998. See: www.timenews.com. Giussani is the head of online strategy at the World Economic Forum.

8. James R. Evans and William M. Lindsay, *The Management and Control of Quality* (West, 1996), pp. 199 – 202.

9. Interview with author, February 1998. Before founding her own firm in 1999, Cannon was executive vice president of Database Marketing Inc., named one of the 500 fastest growing companies by *Inc. Magazine* in 1997. She is a recipient of both the Xplorer of the Year and the Xplor President's Award.

10. Dava Sobel, *Longitude: The Story of a Lone Genius Who Solved the Greatest Scientific Problem of his Time* (Penguin, 1995), pp. 1 - 10.

Chapter Four

1. Xplor International named the State of Wisconsin "Innovator of the Year" in 1997.

2. Interview with author, January 2000. Also: Sandy Kreul, "The Management Challenge," *Document Processing Technology,* June 1999, pp. 20 – 21.

3. James R. Evans and William M. Lindsay, *The Management and Control of Quality* (West, 1996), p. 305. Ken Black, *Business Statistics: Contemporary Decision-Making* (West, 1997), p. 901. Pareto analysis, a system of measures and histograms, is used in the field of Total Quality Management to determine the most salient problems or areas for improvement.

4. Interview with author, February 1998.

5. Interview with author, February 1998.

6. David P. Hanna, *Designing Organizations for High Performance* (Addison-Wesley, 1988), p. 39.

7. Richard A. Quinn, "Converting Vision into Value:

Integrating Business Strategies and Corporate Culture," *Document Processing Technology*, October 1999, pp. 17 – 20. Quinn is also the president of Eskimo Management Company.

8. Xplor International 1999 Technology Directions Survey, p. 40. Xplor International 1998 Technology Directions Survey, p. 36

9. Interview with author, February 1998.

10. Michael Turton, "Document Strategy: So Who's Involved?" *Document Processing Technology*, August 1999, pp. 12 – 14.

11. Interview with author, February 2000. Telles is the former director of communications for the Business Forms Management Association.

Chapter Five

1. Interview with author, March 2000. American Freightways (over $1 billion in annual revenue) is a scheduled, for-hire carrier of general commodities that serves 28 states.

2. Interview with author, April 2000.

3. Adapted from: James R. Evans and William M. Lindsay, *The Management and Control of Quality* (West, 1996), p. 351.

4. Adapted from: Richard Y. Chang, *Measuring Organizational Improvement Impact* (Chang and Associates, 1995).

5. Evans and Lindsay, p. 287.

6. Adapted from: Richard Y. Chang, *Step-By-Step Problem Solving* (Chang and Associates, 1993).

7. Interview with author, February 1998.

8. Adapted from: Richard Y. Chang, *Continuous Process Improvement* (Chang and Associates, 1994).

9. Adapted from: P. Keith Kelly, *Team Decision-Making Techniques* (Chang and Associates, 1994).

Chapter Six

1. Interview with author, April 1998. Nickoloff was a vice president with Kodak before founding planetprint.com. He also serves on the board of the International Publishing Management Association (IPMA).

2. Excel will sometimes require you to enter an IRR guess to complete the calculation. If no guess is entered, a default value of 10% is used.

3. Interview with author, February 1998.

4. Interview with author, February 1998.

5. Adapted from: Daryl R. Conner, *Managing at the Speed of Change: How Resilient Managers Succeed and Prosper Where Others Fail* (Villard, 1993).

6. Interview with author, April 2000. Lietuvnikas was vice chairman of the American Board of Directors for Xplor International in 1998 and 1999.

7. Recommended: Conner, *Managing at the Speed of Change*, and Ralph L. Kliem and Irwin S. Ludin, *Managing Change in the Workplace: A 12-Step Program for Success* (HNB Publishing, 1999).

8. Thanks to Leslie Smid for her contributions to this chapter.

9. Roger Von Oech is the author of *A Kick in the Seat of the Pants* (Harper Collins, 1986) and *A Whack in the Side of the Head* (Warner Books, 1998).

10. Elisabeth Kubler-Ross, *On Death and Dying* (Collier-Macmillan, 1969).

11. Ibid. p. 86.

12. Michael Hammer and James Champy, *Reengineering the Corporation* (Harper Business, 1993), pp. 200 – 213.

13. Adapted from: Bernadette Senn, John Childress and Larry Senn, *Leadership, Teambuilding and Culture Change* (Leadership Press, 1994), p. 73.

14. Ibid. p. 76.

15. Ibid. p. 84.

Chapter Seven

1. Recommended: Eric Verzuh, *The Fast Forward MBA in Project Management* (Wiley and Sons, 1999), and Kathryn P. Rea and Bennet P. Lientz, *Breakthrough Technology Management* (Academic Press, 1998).

2. Recommended: Stephen L. Nelson, et al., *Effective Executive's Guide to Project 2000: The Eight Steps for Using Microsoft Project 2000 to Organize, Manage and Finish Critically Important Projects* (Independent Publishing Group, 2000).

3. Recommended: Geary A. Rummler and Alan P. Brache, *Improving Performance: How to Manage the White Space on the Organizational Chart* (Jossey-Bass, 1995).

4. Adapted from: John J. Cabarro, *Some Preliminary Thoughts on Action Planning and Implementation*, Harvard Business School note number 478-027, 1994.

5. Adapted from: Richard Chang, et al., *Managing Projects Effectively* (Chang and Associates, 1995).

The Author

Kevin Craine has worked in the field of information processing for over 20 years and is currently the manager of document services for Regence BlueCross BlueShield of Oregon and Regence BlueShield in Washington. He is also the editor of Document Processing Technology magazine, and a respected speaker and authority in the disciplines of process improvement, document processing and business technology. He received his BA in organizational communications and his MBA in the management of science and technology.

Visit www.document-strategy.com

This web site is the place to visit for onging support and discussion regarding the design of a document strategy. Based on the book "Designing a Document Strategy," by Kevin Craine, the web site provides a summary and outline of the book, chapter samples and a mailing list registration. As a member of the mailing list you will also have access to ongoing discusson, research and white papers that deal with the varied approaches and complicated issues surrounding the design of document strategy.

The need to implement a document strategy is a topic pursued with urgency in the field of information processing. But in spite of the industry buzz surrounding the subject, the inevitable lament is: "I know a document strategy is important, but how do I actually develop one?" The book, and the accompanying web site, provides a method and process to follow. As a result, whatever decisions and recommendations you ultimately make, they will be more likely to bring about real-world, bottom-line benefits.

Join the growing number of information professionals on the leading edge of document strategy design.

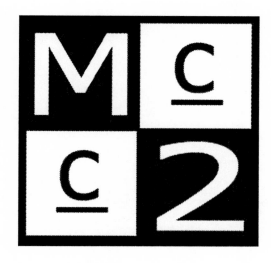

MC^2 Publishing
McGrew + McDaniel Group, Inc.
860 Airport Freeway West   Suite 709
Hurst, Texas 76054

Voice: +1 817 577 8984
Fax: +1 817 577 9371
Email: info@mcgrewmcdaniel.com
URL: www.mcgrewmcdaniel.com

For more information on this title or other titles from MC2, please contact us!

Other titles available from MC2 Publishing in Fall 2000 include:

Critial Mass: A Primer for Living with the Future by P.C. McGrew & W.D. McDaniel

Analog to Digital: What You Need to Know to Get Legacy Data to the Web by P.C. McGrew & W.D. McDaniel

Watch our web site for new titles.

Printed in the United Kingdom
by Lightning Source UK Ltd.
119677UK00001BB/23